CULTURE SMART!
OMAN

Simone Nowell

·K·U·P·E·R·A·R·D·

First published in Great Britain 2009
by Kuperard, an imprint of Bravo Ltd
59 Hutton Grove, London N12 8DS
Tel: +44 (0) 20 8446 2440   Fax: +44 (0) 20 8446 2441
www.culturesmartguides.com
Inquiries: sales@kuperard.co.uk

Culture Smart! is a registered trademark of Bravo Ltd

Distributed in the United States and Canada
by Random House Distribution Services
1745 Broadway, New York, NY 10019
Tel: +1 (212) 572-2844   Fax: +1 (212) 572-4961
Inquiries: csorders@randomhouse.com

Copyright © 2009 Kuperard

Series Editor Geoffrey Chesler
Design Bobby Birchall

ISBN 978 1 85733 475 3

British Library Cataloguing in Publication Data
A CIP catalogue entry for this book is available from the
British Library

Printed in Malaysia

This book is available for special discounts for bulk purchases
for sales promotions or premiums. Special editions, including
personalized covers, excerpts of existing books, and corporate
imprints, can be created in large quantities for special needs.

For more information in the USA write to Special
Markets/Premium Sales, 1745 Broadway, MD 6–2, New York,
NY 10019, or e-mail specialmarkets@randomhouse.com.

In the United Kingdom contact Kuperard publishers at the
address at the top of this page.

About the Author

SIMONE NOWELL is a writer who has spent eleven years in Oman and has traveled extensively throughout the country. Along with her family, she embraced the local culture and made many Omani friends. British by birth, Simone has spent the last twenty-six years in the Middle East and has planted firm roots in the region. Swapping the fast-paced life of the editor of a regional magazine for a slightly slower pace of a freelance author, Simone also encourages local literature and supports the talents of locally-based writers and illustrators through her family's small publishing company. She currently lives in Dubai with her husband, Rashid, and their two children.

The Culture Smart! series is continuing to expand.
For further information and latest titles visit
www.culturesmartguides.com

The publishers would like to thank **CultureSmart!**Consulting for its help in researching and developing the concept for this series.

CultureSmart!Consulting creates tailor-made seminars and consultancy programs to meet a wide range of corporate, public-sector, and individual needs. Whether delivering courses on multicultural team building in the USA, preparing Chinese engineers for a posting in Europe, training call-center staff in India, or raising the awareness of police forces to the needs of diverse ethnic communities, it provides essential, practical, and powerful skills worldwide to an increasingly international workforce.

For details, visit www.culturesmartconsulting.com

CultureSmart!Consulting and **CultureSmart!** guides have both contributed to and featured regularly in the weekly travel program "Fast Track" on BBC World TV.

contents

contents

Map of Oman

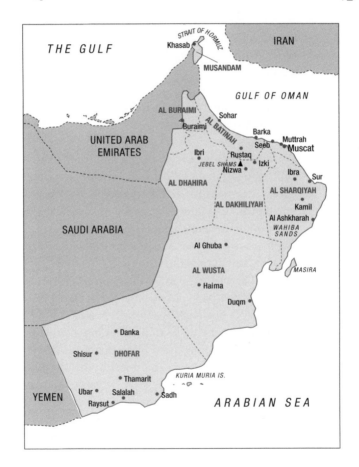

introduction

The Sultanate of Oman, long regarded as one of the more mysterious countries of the Arabian Peninsula, has only recently opened its doors to tourists. An ancient land, with a rich history, dramatic landscape, and diverse flora and fauna, Oman was largely cut off from the modern world until the accession to the throne of Sultan Qaboos in 1970. Since then this peaceful country has developed slowly but deliberately, placing a strong emphasis on retaining its cultural heritage while moving into the high-tech era. Oman is home to Ibadhism, a conservative but moderate form of Islam that is quite distinct from both the Sunni and the Shi'a denominations.

In Oman, the family comes before all else. People place great value on the time they can spend at home, and in relaxing and socializing with friends. Their gentle pace of life contrasts strongly with life in the West, and is reflected in the way they conduct business. Traditional Arabic culture coexists cheerfully with all the trappings of modern life. Flashing neon signs, luxurious new cars, and cell phones are all there, but the call to prayer is heard on virtually every street corner, and national dress is worn throughout the country.

Oman's coastal cities have always been outward-looking, their fleets trading goods and ideas with Mesopotamia, Persia, India, and Africa. Because of its great wealth and strategic position, throughout its history this country has been coveted and conquered by a succession of empires, each leaving its own unique mark, and from the seventeenth to the nineteenth centuries it ruled an East African empire of its own that included the island of Zanzibar.

In the more rural areas Omani life continues much as it has always done. Agriculture continues to play an important role in the economy, alongside the new industries associated with the oil and gas that were discovered in the 1960s. Omanis are employed in all sectors of the economy.

Culture Smart! Oman describes the changing way of life of the Omani people. A historical overview shows how this former maritime trading power rose to prominence and explains the origins of many current Omani social attitudes. By examining the values, customs, and traditions of this distinctly Arabic country, it offers an insight into modern Omani life and culture—how they work and live, both in business and at home, and how they are reacting to their new influx of foreign visitors.

Whether you visit Oman for business, or to explore its unique landscape of mountains, *wadis*, deserts, and beaches, or to discover its other attractions—historic heritage and festivals, shopping and *souqs*, camel races and sand skiing—you will find the Omanis to be a gentle, warm, and hospitable people, who are happy to show their beautiful country to those who treat it with respect. *Ahlan wa sahlan bikum fi Oman!* "Welcome to Oman!"

Key Facts

Official Name	Sultanate of Oman (*Saltanat Uman*)	Oman is a member of the Gulf Cooperation Council (GCC) and a member of the Arab League.
Capital City	Muscat	Population approximately 700,000
Main Cities	Muttrah, Salalah, Nizwa, Sohar, Sur	
Population	2.8 million (2006 estimate)	Pop. growth rate 3.2 % (2007 est.)
Ethnic Makeup	Omani 72%; expatriate workers and GCC nationals 28 %	
Age Structure	0-14 years: 42.7 %; 15-64 years: 54.5 %; 65 years and over: 2.8 %	
Area	119,500 sq. miles (309,500 sq. km)	
Geography	Southeastern corner of the Arabian Peninsula. Bordered by United Arab Emirates, Yemen, and Saudi Arabia	Nine governorates and regions: Muscat, Dhofar, Musandam, Buraimi, Batinah, Ad Dhahirah, Dakhiliyah, Sharqiyah, and Wusta
Terrain	Desert plain, mountain ranges, and coastal plain	1,300 miles (2,092 km) of coastline
Natural Resources	Petroleum, natural gas, chromite, dolomite, zinc, limestone, gypsum, silicon, copper, gold, cobalt, and iron	

Climate	Hot, humid summers (May to September) and mild winters (October to April)	
Currency	Omani Rial (RO or OR)	
Language	Arabic	English is widely spoken, as well as Urdu, Hindi, and Baluchi.
Religion	Ibadhi Islam	
Minority Faiths	Shi'a Islam, Sunni Islam, Christianity, and Hinduism	
Government	Oman is a monarchy	The Sultan is head of state and head of government.
Media	Local television stations and some local newspapers are state owned. There are many privately owned publications.	Main Arabic dailies are *Al Shabiba*, *Al Watan*, *Azzamn*, and *Oman Arabic Daily*. English dailies are *Oman Daily Observer*, *Oman Tribune*, and *Times of Oman*.
Electricity	220 volts (50 Hz)	Sockets designed for 3-pronged plugs but many appliances sold with 2-pronged plugs. Adapters are widely available.
DVD/Video	PAL system	DVD players are usually multiregion.
Telephone	Oman's country code is 968.	To dial out, dial 00 followed by the code.
Internet Domain	.om	
Time Zone	GMT+3 hours	During the summer, GMT+4 hours

chapter one

LAND & PEOPLE

GEOGRAPHY

The Sultanate of Oman is located on the southeast coast of the Arabian Peninsula, with coastlines on the Gulf of Oman and the Arabian Sea. Strategically located on the Strait of Hormuz, directly opposite Iran, it is bordered by three other Middle Eastern countries: the United Arab Emirates to the northwest, Saudi Arabia to the west, and Yemen to the south. It covers an area of 119,500 sq. miles (approximately 309,500 sq. km) and is the second-largest Middle Eastern country after Saudi Arabia. Muscat, the capital, lies on the northeast coast. The main town in the southern Dhofar region is Salalah, also on the coast.

Oman has three distinct geographical regions —coastal plains, mountain range, and plateau— and is home to some of the most varied landscape in the Middle East. The southern coast is lush and green for most of the year, while the Wahiba Sands of the empty quarter remain hot and dry. The coastal cities enjoy both the cooler months of winter and the benefits of trade. One of Oman's particular features is its natural attractions, such as the majestic Jebel Shams mountain range—with its highest point at 9,777 feet (2,980 meters), there is often snow on the summit.

CLIMATE

Oman has only two proper seasons; the hot, humid summer, and the cool winter. Summer starts in May and continues through to September; it is scorching, with temperatures up to 115°F (46°C) during the day, with the addition of humidity ranging from 60 to 80 percent, which is most keenly felt in the coastal towns. However, the southern parts of Oman are far cooler in the summer as they are affected by the monsoon, with temperatures of 84°F (29°C) during the day and

68°F (20°C) at night. Winter, from October to April, is far cooler, with temperatures of 73°F (23°C) during the day and 59°F (15°C) at night.

The annual rainfall in Muscat is approximately 4 inches (10 cm). The Dhofar region has a much heavier annual rainfall of 25 inches (64 cm), which occurs in the summer when the monsoons bring temperatures down and turn the area green.

Shamals (sandstorms) can occur throughout the year, with winds as strong as 30 knots, but are more frequent toward the end of the winter months. These storms can last from one to three days and tend to rage during the day and die out at nightfall. High winds cause low visibility, disrupting everything and everyone from flights out of the airport to the shipping industry and the local shopkeepers at the *souq*. The fine dust penetrates the smallest of cracks around doors and windows, covering everything with a powdery layer.

THE PEOPLE
Oman has a total population of three million, made up of Omanis and approximately 700,000 foreigners. The country enjoys a notably high population growth rate compared with its neighbors—about 3 percent per annum. Around 80 percent of people live in urban settings, with

the rest living in the more rural areas. Much of the workforce in industries such as construction, oil, and gas is made up of foreigners, who tend to live in the larger cities.

As there are many different tribes in Oman, it is difficult to give exact figures for Bedouin or desert dwellers, as they do not all take part in the national census. The Bedouin of Oman are generally nomadic–pastoral, with a minority being nomadic–agricultural. People in rural areas are usually engaged in agriculture, such as date farming and frankincense harvesting; much of the region's pottery and handicrafts also comes from these areas.

A BRIEF HISTORY
Prehistory

The Omani people are very conscious of their national history, which they learn in school, and the history of their tribe, both of which form an important part of an individual's identity.

Archaeological excavations along the south-eastern fringes of the Arabian Peninsula show that human civilization in Oman is very ancient. In the twelfth millennium BCE the world was just emerging from the last Ice Age, and the area was greener and more humid than today. The earliest Omanis lived in the mountain valleys and survived by hunting gazelle, wild cattle, and other animals, which were plentiful. Their stone weapons and tools included knives, awls, and drills that were comparatively advanced and of high quality; examples have been found in Dhofar, Wadi Bahla, lzki, lbra, and along the northern Omani coasts.

The picture archaeologists have drawn of Oman, prior to written records, is one of settled life in towns and villages scattered along riverbanks and in mountain valleys, where water was readily available. During that period the people built stone houses, made beautifully decorated clay utensils, as well as dishes and cups of stone and alabaster, wore woven clothes, and adorned themselves with jewelry. They traveled widely by donkey and perhaps camel, as these were domesticated at that time. The remains of ancient villages and towns show that they built roads between lbra and Buraimi and the Omani coast.

The Seafaring State of Majan

The contents of tombs discovered near Buraimi, lbra, and other sites on the Omani coast show

cultural and commercial contact between Oman
and Iraq, Persia, and India. By the second half of
the third millennium BCE, there was extensive
commercial activity between Oman and Persia,
India, and Mesopotamia. Early writings
from this era mention these
countries, their goods, and
commercial activities. They
also refer repeatedly to
"Majan," which, say
archaeologists, is the country
we know today as Oman, but
which then also included the whole
Gulf coast. Babylonian and Sumerian records
mention that King Sargon of Akkad (2371–2316
BCE) prided himself on the fact that ships from
Majan and Delmoon (modern-day Bahrain)
came to dock in his ports and harbors. Two
centuries later, Ur-Namu (2113–2096 BCE), King
of Ur, claimed that he had won back the ships of
Majan—probably by offering favorable
commercial relations to Majan, or by improving
his own ports. The Akkadian King Naram Sin
(2225–2191 BCE), for unknown reasons, actually
invaded and occupied Majan. However, Majan's
King Manium was treated with honor and
respect, and the Sumerian town of Maniumiki
was even named after him.

From these historical events and the fact that the Omanis were among the first people to sail across the warm waters of the Gulf, we can conclude that Oman's prosperity was due mainly to its judicious use of its strategic location, within reach of India, Persia, Iraq, and Africa. Majan was also known in this period as "Jabal Al Nihas" (the copper mountain). Copper was one of the main commodities carried by its ships, and Oman has numerous ancient copper mines. Laboratory tests have demonstrated that old Omani copper from the Sohar Mountains contains nickel, as does the copper found in the Sumerian town of Ur in modern Iraq. Timber is also mentioned in the export records of Majan, and recent research has shown that a large area of Oman was forested.

Civilization from the First Millennium BCE

After the prosperity of the third millennium BCE, Oman's history during the second millennium BCE is shrouded in obscurity. So far nothing significant has been found to give a clear picture of life in the region during this period. Trade between Majan, Delmoon, and Milokha (India) suddenly ceased around 2000 BCE. Delmoon itself suffered a temporary decline around 1800 BCE.

We have no information on any maritime activities, apart from some indications found in

Buraimi that there were commercial relations between Loristan in Persia and Oman. By the first quarter of the first millennium BCE prosperity had returned to Oman with the rise of the Assyrian civilization. Omani merchants returned to Indian ports, and possibly also to African shores, trading in spices, perfume, and timber from Delmoon, and in copper from Majan itself. However, commerce did not completely recover until the rise of the Achaemenid dynasty in Persia and the invasion of Egypt by the Persian king Cambyses in 525 BCE. His successor, Darius the Great, captured parts of India, restoring to the Gulf the maritime trade it had lost to the Red Sea, where Phoenician commerce flourished.

In 325 BCE, Admiral Nearchus sailed with Alexander the Great from India. In his diary he

wrote about a port in the Arabian Peninsula named Mekitah. This was probably Rass Musandam, whence "cinnamon and other goods were shipped to Assyria." It seems that in the third century BCE a sea route was opened up between Oman and Taborban (today's Sri Lanka), the source of cinnamon, and while there Omani merchants also traded for gold imported from the Far East.

Oman and the Early Arabs
Arabs have always inhabited Oman. The ancient tribe of Add is known to have lived in the sand dunes between Oman and Hadramaut to its west. The Greek geographer and historian Strabo (c. 63 BCE–21 CE) wrote that the Arab tribe of "Thamood" had also lived in this region. Other Arab tribes gave their names to Omani regions. The port city of Sohar, for example, is named after the Sohar tribe, who lived in the region of Batinah, and the name of the Obal tribe is recalled in the name of a valley that lies between Ruwaha and Rustaq. According to Arab genealogists, Sam Bin Noah ruled the region between Hijaz in northwest Arabia and Oman. His grandson, Suhail, built Sohar.

In about the eighth century BCE, Yarub Bin Qahtan, head of the Yarub tribe in southwest Arabia, extended their rule to other parts of the peninsula. He sent his brothers to govern Oman, Hadramut, and Hijaz. The great thirteenth-century historian Ibn Khaldun wrote, "Yarub Bin Qahtan was one of the greatest kings on earth. It is said that he was the first to receive a royal salute from his people. He ruled over the Yemen, vanquished the people of Add and the Amaliqa of the Hijaz. He appointed his brothers governors of all these regions. Jarham ruled in Hijaz, Add Bin Qahtan in Al Shahr, Hadramut Bin Qahtan in Jibal Al Shammar and Oman Bin Qahtan in Arabia."

Yarub's successor, Yashjib, lost his hold on Oman, but this was regained by his son, Abd Shams, who governed all the regions to the south of the Arabian Peninsula. The Himyarit dynasty, which is descended from him, ruled the Yemen from 115 BCE until the advent of Islam. Oman, under the rule of the legendary kingdom of Sheba (Saba'a), had close relations with the neighboring Himyarati kingdom.

In the middle of the sixth century BCE, the Persian Achaemenids, under Cyrus the Great, invaded Oman and exerted control over the country from the coast. Oman's underground irrigation canals (*aflaj*) were probably constructed during this period. Northern Oman would remain under the control of successive Persian dynasties until around 800 CE.

The Azd Migration

Obscurity surrounds events in Oman in the period between Achaemenid (sixth to fourth century BCE) and Sassanid Persian rule (226–640 CE), but part of the country was still under Persian rule at the time of the great Azd migration from Yemen to Oman, under the leadership of Malik Bin Fahm. This migration took place just after the collapse of the Great Dam of Marib in Yemen in the sixth century CE, which caused great social disruption and resulted in the mass exodus of an estimated 50,000 people. While the Marib dam had been regularly breached by local flooding, this catastrophic final breach has been attributed to lack of repair and maintenance. A flash flood resulted in the complete destruction of the dam and its associated irrigation network, bringing an end to an ancient civilization.

The early migrations of the Azd were chronicled by the eighteenth-century Omani historian Sirhan Bin Sa'id. He gives a detailed account of the story of Malik Bin Fahm, who appointed his son, Han'a, to lead the Azd army. When they arrived in Oman, Malik sent a messenger to Al Mazraban, the Persian governor, asking for permission to settle in a region with access to water and grazing. The Persians decided "not to allow this Arab to settle among them.

They thought 'their land' was too small, even for themselves." Both parties prepared for war on the plain near Nizwa, and after a fierce battle Oman was liberated and Malik became the ruler.

Arab historians record that the Azd were the kings of the mountains and the deserts. The treaty with the Persians now gave them full sovereignty. The Sassanids called the Azd leaders "Al Jalandi," the title by which all future Omani rulers were known.

Oman—the Name

It is said that the Azd gave the name Oman to the country because the valley they settled in resembled a valley called Oman in their ancestral Marib. The Persians called the land Mazona. Some believe that Oman was named after Oman Bin Ibrahim Al Khalil, others that it was named after the founder of the country, Oman Bin Seba Bin Yafthan Bin Ibrahim Khalil Al Rahman. Historians have even linked "Oman" linguistically to a word meaning "settling" or "staying." Whatever the origin of its name, there is no doubt that before the coming of the Yemeni Qahtani and the northern Adnani Arabs, Oman was inhabited by Arab races that no longer exist, such as the Add, who lived in the Ahqaf area between Oman and Hadramut, and the Tassam and Jadees, who lived in Yamama, east of Najd.

Early Omani Muslims

Oman embraced Islam during the
Prophet Mohammed's lifetime (that is,
before 632 CE). At the time the country was
ruled by the Jalandi dynasty. According to some
historians, it was converted during the reign of Al
Jalandi Bin Al Mustansir, who died a year later.
Others say that Bin Al Mustansir never lived to see
Islam, and that an emissary of the Prophet, Amr Bin
Al As, was sent to Oman in 630 CE carrying this
message to the sons of Bin Al Mustansir, Abd and
Jayfar, who together ruled the country: "In the name
of Allah, the Merciful and Compassionate. From the
messenger of Allah to Jayfar and Abd, the two sons
of Al Jalandi. Peace be upon those who follow the
righteous cause. I call upon you to embrace Islam.
Be Muslims and be saved. I am sent by Allah to all
peoples to warn the living that punishment will be
meted out to the unbelievers. If you embrace Islam,
I shall confirm you as rulers. If you deny Islam your
kingdom will vanish, my horses will be at your gate
and my prophecies will destroy your kingdom."

Abd and Jayfar converted to Islam. They
summoned the chiefs of the tribes and presented
them with this fact. The people then flocked to join
them, and Oman was absorbed into the Caliphate.
Many historical accounts show that the Prophet
devoted special attention to Oman.

THE PROPHET'S BLESSING

The first Omani to embrace Islam, according to Arab historians, was Mazin Bin Ghadhuba Bin Subaya Bin Shamasa. He went to the Prophet and declared his faith, whereupon the Prophet prayed for him and for the people of Oman and blessed them. Mazin then went out to preach and call on the people to join the new faith.

Al Atbi gave an account of the meeting between the Prophet and Mazin Bin Ghadhuba. Mazin said to the Prophet, "Oh, Messenger of Allah, pray for the people of Oman." The Prophet replied, "Oh, Allah, show them the light and make them firm in their faith." Mazin said, "More, oh Messenger of Allah," and the Prophet said, "Oh, Allah, give them chastity, contentment, and satisfaction with your gifts." Mazin said, "Messenger of Allah, the sea is by our side. Pray to Allah to protect our supplies, camels, and cattle." The Prophet prayed, "Oh, God, show them your bounty and increase their provisions from the sea." Mazin said, "More." The Prophet added, "Oh, God, do not make them subject to foreign enemies." The Prophet turned to Mazin and said, "Oh, Mazin, say Amen, for

with this word the prayer may be answered."
And then Mazin said, "Amen."

The following year Mazin returned to the
Prophet, and said, "Blessed you are and the
son of the blessed. Good you are and son of
the good. God has led more people of Oman
and guided them to your faith. Oman has
increased its harvests and catches of fish." The
Prophet said, "My faith is the faith of Islam
and the Almighty will give the people of
Oman greater harvests and more fish. Blessed
are those who believed in me and beheld me.
Blessed are those who believed in me without
seeing me and blessed are those who believed
in me and have not seen Him who saw me.
The Almighty Allah will increase the faith
of Oman."

**Oman and the Cultural Movement at the
Dawn of Islam**

After embracing Islam, the Omanis
enthusiastically studied the Koran, its
interpretation, the Arabic language, and its
literature. Oman, by virtue of its many religious
scholars, became a leading cultural center in the
Islamic world. While *faqihs* (religious scholars), by

definition, specialize in Islamic law and religious studies, it is worth noting that no real distinctions were drawn at the time between the scholars of different intellectual disciplines. The Omanis were involved in every aspect of learning.

Given that Oman had an ancient civilization, it was no surprise that it became an important nation with the advent of Islam. Oman was the cradle of great men of science, orators, and scholars. The ninth-century writer Al Jahidh is reported to have said, "I may have heard the ignorant saying: what do the Omanis know? But where else are so many scholars and orators like Musqala Bin Al Raqia, the best of the orators, and his son Karb Bin Musqala?"

In every Arab history book, mention is made of Oman's men of learning. The most famous of the Omani *qadis* (judges) was Ka'ab Bin Siwar, who was appointed supreme judge in Basrah by the second caliph Omar Bin Khattab (c. 581–83). Among its greatest scientists were Abu Sha'tha Jabir Bin Zaid Al Azdi, Sohar Bin Abbas, Al Rabie Bin Habib (a contemporary of Jabir Bin Zaid, an Omani scholar and intellectual, and some say the first Imam and Founder of Ibadhism), Abu Al

Mundir Bashir Al Mundir Al Nizwani, and many
others. Oman's impressive scientific tradition
continues largely unbroken to this day.

Oman and the Islamic Conquests

The Omanis were active in spreading Islam.
According to some sources King Abd Bin Jalandi
obtained Caliph Abu Bakr's permission to raise an
army against the Gassanis in Syria. The Omanis,
in particular, played a decisive role in the
conquest of the Maghreb (North Africa), and in
the spread of Islam in Africa as a whole. Although
foreign and Arabic contemporary sources paid
little attention to them, lbadhi preachers from
Oman were active among the Berber tribes and
suffered great hardship in spreading the word of
Islam. The history of lbadhism in the Maghreb is
a clear pointer to links with the Middle East,
which were forged by the lbadhi scholars.

Sohar—Marketplace of the World

In the early days of Islam Oman continued to be
ruled by the Al Jalandi dynasty. They later
recaptured the port of Sohar and the surrounding
arable lands and won back virtually all the
maritime concessions that the Persians had
enjoyed. It was then that the Al Jalandi acquired
the fortress of Huzu in Persia, overlooking the

Gulf, and collected taxes from ships passing through their sphere of influence.

After it was retaken by the Omanis, Sohar preserved its status as an important trading port. However, its golden age did not really begin until Oman gained full independence (943–53) from the centralized power exercised by the Abbasid Caliphate in Baghdad. Al Jalandi rulers kept their control of the fortress of Huzu while the Omani mercantile fleet sailed to Africa and Madagascar to buy ivory, wool, tiger skins, and amber, which were very much in demand in Iraq, India, and China. According to reports by contemporary travelers Sohar was by then the leading trading port in the Gulf.

According to the Persian author of the book *Hudood al-Alam*, Sohar was ". . . the marketplace of the world . . . its traders are certainly the richest in the world. Goods from north, south, east and west are brought here and then distributed to other parts of the world." The eleventh-century Arab historian Al Maqdasi, living in the time of Sohar's prosperity, paints the following picture: "No town in the China Sea is larger than [Sohar]. It is populous, beautiful and affluent. Along its coast are wondrous shops and magnificent houses built of bricks and teak. Through it runs a canal of fresh water. Sohar is the gateway to China, the storehouse of Iraq and the East, and a stopping-place on the road to Yemen."

The Imamate of Oman (751–1154)

In the latter days of their rule, the Umayyad Caliphs based in Damascus transformed the principle of rule in Islam from that of consultation (*Shura*) to hereditary monarchy. In opposition to this, the Omanis embraced the lbadhi sect of Islam, which adopts the principle of *Shura* as laid down by the Prophet and his two successors. Ibadi spiritual leaders, or Imams, are nominated by the *ulama* (the religious scholars) and confirmed in office by a public oath of allegiance. The internal strife experienced by the Azd of Oman and Iraq during the first third of the eighth century provided a strong incentive for the Omanis to embrace lbadhism, whose leaders advocated a return to true Islamic values.

After the downfall of the Ummayad Caliphate in 750 CE, the coastal regions of Oman were once more exposed to attack by external powers. In the interior, however, the Omanis succeeded in establishing an independent state called the Imamate of Oman. The elective office of Imam passed from tribe to tribe. The capital of the Imamate, too, moved from one town to another, but mostly remained in Nizwa and Rustaq. The

Imam assumed full or partial spiritual, political, and military authority, as dictated by the circumstances.

The Imam, as indicated by his title, was the spiritual head who led the faithful in Friday prayer, and was the highest authority in all religious matters. He was also responsible for all civil affairs, such as the collection of taxes. He commanded the army in time of war, if he was fit, and in any case the decision to go to war or to cease hostilities was his alone. However, his authority was always restricted by tribal strife on the one hand, and by the philosophy of lbadhism on the other.

From the beginning of the reign of Warith Bin Ka'ab, and for a period of a hundred years until 887, the Omanis successfully repulsed both the armies of the Abbasid Caliph of Baghdad and pirates from India. This success was due chiefly to the power of their fleet, whose main vessels were built during the reign of Imam Ghassan Bin Abdullah (807–24).

Foreign Invasions

After Imam Al Salt Bin Malik was deposed, there was a polarization of support for either the Nizari faction in the north, or the Yamani faction of Bedouin in the south. The former appealed for assistance to the Caliph Al Mua'tadid (892–902), who sent the governor of Bahrain, Muhammad Bin Noor, in command of a Nizari army of 25,000 to Oman. In 893 the country was overrun by the army of Bin Noor. These were black days. In the words of the Omani historian Sirhan Bin Said, "Thus Oman was wrested from the hands of its people and brought under the rule of Muhammad Bin Noor, a rule of terror and oppression . . . The invaders amputated hands, feet and ears of their victims . . . gouged out their eyes . . . blocked the irrigation channels . . . and burned the books of Ibadhism."

When Muhammad Bin Noor withdrew from Oman he left the country in the hands of Ahmed Bin Helal. He, however, looked after the interests of the Omani people and encouraged trade, especially after moving his capital from Bahla to Sohar. He defended his capital against the ambitions of Caliph Al Muktadir (908–932). With the weakening of the central Caliphate in Baghdad, the proclamation of independence by Egypt and Syria, and the declaration of self-rule by the Walis in Khurasan (Persia), the Omanis once more had the opportunity to rebuild their country and develop its trade.

In 929, Abu Tahir Al Kurmuti of Basrah occupied Oman. The lbadhis found the Kurmutis, who practiced social reform and justice, the most enlightened of the foreign powers to occupy Oman. This state of affairs lasted until 985 and, despite paying tax to the Kurmutis, Oman enjoyed thirty-five years of total independence from Baghdad.

During this period, the port of Sohar became the greatest in the Islamic world. The Omani merchant fleet, with its great naval history, voyaged to the shores of Africa, Madagascar, and the Far East. Although the Jalandi dynasty had lost direct control over Oman at this period, they collected taxes from the ships passing through the Gulf close to their stronghold of Huzu, where they minted their own coins bearing the name of Radwan Bin Ja'afar, master of the seas and commander of the fortress. So great were Oman's maritime and mercantile powers that, as one historian has put it, in the tenth century the Omanis ruled the waves of the Indian Ocean.

The fortunes amassed by Omani traders in Iraq and southern Persia roused the envy of their region's ruler, Muiz Al Dawla Al Buwayhi. In 965 he sent his fleet, under the command of Abu Al Faraj Muhammad Bin Abbas, to Oman. The Persian fleet landed at Julfar (Ras Al Khaimah), arriving in Sohar in 971, where the invaders massacred most of the population. They ravaged towns and villages, killed great numbers of people, and burned seventy-nine merchant ships. Soon after, the last Jalandi ruler was killed at Huzu.

Buwayhid rule lasted only a hundred years before it was overthrown by the Seljuk Turks, who occupied Oman in 1064. With the coming of the Seljuks, Oman, especially the coastal regions, was about to witness three hundred years of anarchy. Seljuki rule lasted no more than eighty years, and was followed by attacks on Oman by armies and pirates from Basrah, Khurasan, and Persia.

Dual Rule with the Nabhani

In the mid-twelfth century, the Beni Nabhan tribe proclaimed independence from the Imamate and announced a hereditary monarchy, which lasted until the fifteenth century. The rivalry between elected imam and hereditary king would now become a feature of Omani history. The country was suffering from internal divisions and had lost its political unity. This left the coastal towns wide-open to invasion. The Arab historian Abu Al Fida described Sohar in the fourteenth century as "a village razed to the ground."

The fourteenth-century Arab traveler Ibn Battuta visited Oman and wrote about the Beni Nabhan, "The Sultan of Oman is an Arab from the tribe of Azd Bin Al Gouth, known as Abu Muhammad Bin Nabhan. 'Abu Muhammad' is the name they give to any ruler of Oman. This Sultan sits outside his

house with no attendants or ministers around him. Everyone is allowed to approach him, stranger or native. He honors his guests in the Arab tradition and extends to them his hospitality and attention. He is a man of commendable manners."

The Omani historian Sirhan Bin Said wrote that he could find no trace of the imams of Oman during a period of two hundred and fifty years—between 1153, the year of the death of Imam Musa Bin Abu Ja'afar, and 1406, the year of the death of Imam Hubaise Bin Muhammad.

From the fifteenth century to the end of the seventeenth century, power struggles meant that the country had both an imam, elected from among its dignitaries, and a hereditary sultan of the Nabhani dynasty. Certain events mentioned by Arab historians give an indication as to who was holding real power and authority.

The story of Sultan Suleiman Bin Mudhafar Al Nabhani and the Imam Muhammad Ibn Ismail (1500–29) shows that the real power was in the hands of the imam. "Suleiman was alone in his bedroom when he heard a voice saying: 'Enjoy yourself, son of Nabhan, the days of your reign are numbered.' Suleiman took this to be a Satanic whisper. Next morning, while traveling with his two attendants to Nizwa, he saw a woman swimming in a canal. When he accosted her, she ran from him, screaming for help. Imam Muhammad Ibn Ismail rushed to her aid, stabbing Suleiman through the heart."

In 1507 the coastal area, including the port city of Muscat, fell under Portuguese control.

Oman had both elected imams and Nabhani sultans at least until the time of Nasser Bin Murshid, the great Yarubi Imam who took office in 1624. He came to power in a country that was deeply divided, and whose northern ports

had been occupied by the Portuguese for more than a hundred years.

The Yarubi Imamate (1624–1724)

Omani historians say that Imam Nasser Bin Murshid, the founder of the Yarubi dynasty, led the Omani people from the dark days of division, strife, and foreign occupation into "the sunlight of salvation." It was in 1614 that Nasser, after some hesitation, bowed to the wishes of seventy Omani religious leaders (*ulama*) and accepted the Imamate to lead the country. From his base in Rustaq he began the task of unifying the country.

The Portuguese, who occupied the northern coast, including Muscat and Muttrah, seeing the success of the new Imam, hastened to call for peace. This led to a treaty whereby the Portuguese agreed to pay a levy, to allow the Omanis to trade freely, and to refrain from all military action. The Imam held the upper hand, and the agreement did not stop him from liberating the towns of Sur and Quriyat from the Portuguese. He then turned to the Eastern Region in order to complete the unification of the country.

When Imam Nasser died in 1649, his cousin, Sultan Bin Saif, was chosen to take his place. The first thing he did was to drive the Portuguese out of Muscat in 1650, thus completing the liberation of Omani lands. He continued to attack the Portuguese, even at sea, and followed them in his ships to the shores of India. Since then Oman has never suffered another foreign occupation, with the exception of the period between 1737 and 1747, when the Persians interfered in a civil war and occupied parts of the coast.

Oman then started building its relations with foreign countries by agreements and conventions. Even when the British Empire was at its zenith, and controlling the Gulf States through restrictive treaties, Oman was an independent country with privileged relations with Britain.

The glory of the Yarubi dynasty was not built on the liberation of Oman and the foundation of independence alone, but on the fact that their rule ushered in a period of revival and prosperity in all aspects of life. The resurgence of Oman's maritime power paved the way for commercial prosperity, greater wealth, the spread of education, and the construction of magnificent buildings. Whereas the era of Imam Nasser was generally a period of liberation and unification,

the rule of Imam Sultan was characterized by construction and development. He built the grand, circular Saif castle in Nizwa, which took twelve years to complete, and reconstructed the Nizwa–Izki *falaj* (a highly effective irrigation system, still in use today). Much of his attention was devoted to the consolidation of Oman's foreign relations, an essential ingredient for flourishing trade, and he sent emissaries to India, Iran, Yemen, and Iraq.

Imam Sultan's Benevolent Rule

The Omani historian Hamid Bin Muhammad Bin Ruzaik summarized Imam Sultan's achievements and the country's affluence by saying that Oman "flourished under his rule and the people had respite from their wearisome troubles. The roads were safe, goods were cheap, profits high, and crops plentiful. The Imam himself was modest, kind to his subjects, and tolerant of their shortcomings when these did not transgress Islamic codes. He was not distant or haughty to his people. He used to walk the streets without guards, sit with the people, and talk to them without any constraint. He used to greet the old and the young, the free and the slave alike."

Civil War in the Early Eighteenth Century

When Imam Sultan died his son Balarab succeeded him as Imam, and a dispute arose between him and his brother, Saif Bin Sultan. This rivalry led to bitter divisions in the land, to the extent that the people began to call Balarab "*Bala Arab*," meaning "Scourge of the Arabs," and to call his brother Saif "Disaster."

Saif was eventually able to gain control of all the principal fortresses, which gave him power and ensured that he was declared Imam during the life of his brother. After the death of Balarab no one opposed the confirmation of Saif as Imam; indeed, he earned his people's respect through his victories against the Portuguese in their African colonies. When he died in 1711 his son, Imam Sultan Bin Saif II, inherited a prosperous country; but on his death in 1718 the century-long unity of the country came to an end.

At this point, civil war broke out between the Hinawi (descendants of the Qahtan) and the Ghaffiriya (descendants of the Nizar) over the succession to the Imamate. Should Saif II's son Saif be Imam, in line with the long-established hereditary rule, which was supported by the tribal chiefs, or should an Imam be elected, as the *ulama* (religious leaders) upheld?

The dispute continued until 1743, when both chiefs of the warring tribes died—Imam Sultan Bin Murshid Al Yarubi, who in 1741 had been the *ulama's* choice, and Imam Saif Bin Sultan Bin Saif II, who had assumed the Imamate for the second time in 1727 with the consent of his enemies, the Hinawis. On the death of the two imams the struggle took a new course. War broke out between the Persian forces who had come to the aid of Imam Saif, and the Omanis in Sohar under Imam Saif's commander, Ahmed Bin Said. Bin Said displayed courage and ability in defending the town during the Persian siege.

Following an agreement, under which the Persians withdrew from Sohar to Muscat in 1744, Ahmed Bin Said invited the Persian officers to a banquet, during which his troops fell upon them and put them to the sword. Only a few managed to escape to Jelfar in modern day UAE, from where they finally withdrew in 1748. Ahmed Bin Said became a popular hero and was elected Imam in acknowledgment of his resourcefulness, and because no Yarubi contender had come forward after the deaths of Saif and Sultan.

The Al Busaid Family and the Omani Empire
Imam Ahmed Bin Said, "Al Busaid," assumed the Imamate of Oman in 1749. He was able to ride

out clashes with the Yarubi family, who, supported by the Ghafiriyyas, sought to impose their own Imam. He also avoided a clash with his two sons, Saif and Sultan, who opposed his rule. His attention was directed toward the revival of Oman's maritime trade.

During Al Busaid's reign, the Sultanate of Muscat and Oman became a regional and international power to be reckoned with. His naval force made a significant contribution to the stability of the region. In 1756, when the Persians surrounded Basrah, the Wali of Baghdad sought the help of the Imam. He sent an army of ten thousand men aboard a hundred vessels to raise the siege. In recognition of this great victory the Ottoman sultan allocated an annual fund to Oman. In 1775 the Omani fleet consisted of twenty-four warships, four of which carried forty-four cannons, and five frigates, each with eighteen to twenty-four cannons. The remaining ships carried eight to fourteen cannons each.

Imam Ahmed earned the admiration of the Moghul emperor of India, Shah Alam, following the success of his navy in rounding up the pirates who plagued the coasts of India and capturing some of their leaders. Shah Alam and the Imam signed a mutual defense treaty and a Moghul ambassador was appointed to Muscat.

Internally, Imam Ahmed Bin Said established a strong central government, and was known for his tolerance, foresight, and attention to detail. When he died in Rustaq in 1783, his son Said succeeded him as Imam, despite the general desire to have his more capable elder son, Hilal, as his successor; but Hilal, suffering from an eye disease, traveled to Sind, India, to seek a remedy, and never returned.

The new Imam, Said Bin Ahmed, had been unpopular ever since he was Wali of Nizwa, where he had monopolized the trade in indigo and implemented other measures that alienated the people. As a result, high-ranking Omanis attempted to replace him as Imam. First they supported his brother Qays, and later his own son, Hamed, who became the effective ruler of Oman and resided in Muscat while his father stayed in Rustaq. These events led to the separation of the functions of Sultan and Imam, with far-reaching political and social consequences for Oman.

Hamed surrounded himself with scholars, philosophers, and men of wisdom, was renowned for his fairness, and was the first of his family to be given the respectful title "Al Sayed" by his people. He devoted much attention to extending Oman's naval influence. He captured the island of

Lamu off the East African coast and was planning to take Mombasa and even Calcutta, but died suddenly in 1792 and was succeeded by another brother, Sayed Sultan. Oman's influence in the days of Sayed Sultan extended to both sides of the Gulf, and fees were levied from all passing ships.

The latter part of the eighteenth century and the beginning of the nineteenth witnessed continuous regional wars between Sayed Sultan and the seafaring Qawasim tribe, who were joined by their allies the Wahhabis of central Arabia. The Qawasim wanted to increase their share of trade in the Gulf, while Sayed Sultan claimed sole rights over all naval activities in the area.

Rise of the Wahhabi

The rise of the fundamentalist Wahhabi movement in Najd in central Arabia greatly influenced the course of history in the south and east of the Arabian Peninsula. During the last quarter of the eighteenth century, the tribes of Najd found themselves united under the banner of the Wahhabi movement and sought expansion in all directions. In 1800, the Wahhabi captured the Omani region of Buraimi. The Qawasim and the Wahhabi also reached the Batinah coast (the stretch of coastline from Seeb to Sohar) and occupied Barka. However, Sayed Sultan was able to sweep through the Gulf in 1804 with a fleet of fourteen warships. At Basrah he sought the help of his Ottoman allies, but on his return he was attacked and killed by the Qawasim while sailing in a small ship close to Linja, an island off the Persian coast, where he was buried. After his death Oman once more went through a period of confusion and unrest, which came to an end when Sayed Said Bin Sultan Bin Ahmed took control of the situation. He ruled Oman for more than fifty years (1804–56).

Zanzibar and Oman

In 1807 Sayed Said signed a treaty of friendship and trade with De Caen, the French commander general in the East. This agreement did not survive any length of time as the French were expelled from the island of Mauritius by the British. Then Sayed Said forged close ties with the British, which were to last to the end of his reign. Sayed Said

was a capable leader whose aspirations extended beyond Oman's borders toward India, Persia, and

Africa. In the first half of the nineteenth century, the Sultanate of Muscat and Oman was the most powerful state in Arabia.

During his reign, the Omani Empire included the Gulf region, southern Iran, and Baluchistan. Omani territory extended for more than 1,864 miles (3,000 km) along the coast of East Africa, including the ports of Mombasa and Dar es Salaam. The island of Zanzibar was the capital of Oman's African territories, and Zanzibar City one of the richest towns along the East African coast. Sayed Said introduced cloves and other valuable plants into East Africa, and established rich plantations that improved the economy of the coastal towns. The prosperity enjoyed by these regions was maintained even after the opening of the Suez Canal in 1869, which restored the importance of the Red Sea as a trade route at the expense of the Cape of Good Hope. Said died at the age of sixty-two in 1856 on board the vessel *Victoria*, near the Seychelles. He was buried in the garden of his palace in Zanzibar.

The Empire Divided

Sayed's place as ruler of Zanzibar was taken by his son Majid, who confirmed all the official appointments made by his father in the African territories of the empire. Meanwhile, in Muscat, his other son, Thuayni, disputed the succession. With the support of the majority of the Omani people, he declared himself ruler of the entire sultanate. The people of Zanzibar and the Omani African colonies backed Majid's leadership.

In 1861 the dispute between the two brothers was resolved by British arbitration. Majid was made ruler of Zanzibar and the Omani territories in Africa, and Thuayni was declared ruler of Oman proper with the right to receive from Majid an annual contribution of 40,000 guineas in gold. After a short period of disagreement over the terms of the accord, the two sultans were given formal international recognition by Britain and France in a joint declaration issued in Paris in 1862 in which the two superpowers agreed to respect the independence of the two sultanates.

The status of Oman started to decline, as a result of divisions within the sultanate and the loss of most of the vessels of its fleet, which happened to be in Zanzibar when Said died.

Tensions arose between the more conservative tribal regions of the interior and the central government over the respective roles of Sultan and Imam. There was sporadic civil unrest until 1920, when the Treaty of Seib was signed during the reign of Sultan Taimour Bin Faisal. Under the terms of this treaty the disturbances ended and the warring factions were brought together. However, the political compromise did nothing to bring the economy out of recession.

In 1932 Sultan Taimour, having little desire to rule, abdicated in favor of his son Said Bin Taimour, who inherited a debt-ridden state. In the first part of Sultan Said's reign, the treasury reserves dropped to the equivalent of £50,000. Moreover, the country suffered a civil war in Dhofar in the south, which was aggravated by international and regional interference. Sultan Said did manage to restore the country to a stable financial state through austerity measures, but failed to modernize or invest in Oman's future. The austerity measures were retained even after the discovery of oil. On December 20, 1951, a new friendship, trade, and maritime agreement with Britain was signed, which also recognized the full independence of Oman.

On July 23, 1970, Sultan Qaboos Bin Said took over the reins of office with the consent of the entire Omani people, its royal family, and armed forces. He opened the doors of the sultanate to the world in a drive to build a modern state, thus starting the great march forward.

THE HOUSE OF AL BUSAID

- Imam Ahmed Bin Said Bin Ahmed Bin Muhammad Al-Busaidy (1749–83)
- Imam Said Bin Ahmed Bin Said (1783–84)
- Al-Sayed Hamed Bin Said (1784–92)
- Al-Sayed Sultan Bin Ahmed Bin Said (1792–1804)
- Al-Sayed Said Bin Sultan Bin Ahmed (Omani Empire) (1804–56)
- Al-Sayed Thuayni Bin Said Bin Sultan (1856–66)
- Al-Sayed Salim Bin Thuayni Bin Said (1866–68)
- Imam 'Azzan Bin Qais Bin-Azzan Bin Qais Bin Ahmed (1868–71)
- Sultan Turki Bin Said Bin Sultan Ibn-Imam (1871–88)
- Sultan Faisal Bin Turki Bin Said (1888–1913)
- Sultan Taimour Bin Faisal (1913–32)
- Sultan Said Bin Taimour (1932–70)
- Sultan Qaboos Bin Said Al Said (1970–present)

GOVERNMENT AND POLITICS
The Monarch: H. M. Sultan Qaboos Bin Said Al Said (1970–present)

The current ruler of Oman is H. M. Sultan Qaboos Bin Said Al Said, who began his rule in

1970, taking over from his father, H. M. Sultan Said Bin Taimour, after a bloodless coup. Sultan Qaboos has taken Oman from humble beginnings to a country successfully exploiting its natural resources and building a modern infrastructure, while preserving its traditional Islamic roots.

Born on November 18, 1940, and educated in the UK, Sultan Qaboos is the eighth sultan of Oman and is a direct descendant of Al Bu Said. He is revered for his forethought and leadership in the areas of education, literacy, and the elimination of poverty. He has managed to bring Oman into the twenty-first century while ensuring that the social framework of this Islamic society has remained firmly in place.

Sultan Qaboos has, to a certain extent, opened up the government to public participation through the elected members of the Majlis ash-Shura. He undertakes an annual tour of the country lasting several days, taking with him his ministers and other important Omani figures, and meeting with his people.

Legislature and Judiciary
Oman is a monarchy, with the Sultan both head of state and head of government. The government consists of two bodies, provided for by the Basic Statute of State. The Majlis Oman (Council of Oman) is made up of the Majlis ash-Shura (Consultative Shura/Council), whose members are elected by Omani citizens every three years,

and the Majlis a-Dowla (State Council), whose members are appointed by the monarch and represent the governorates and regions of Oman. All members must meet certain conditions, and members are not permitted to sit on both councils. The Majlis a-Dowla has financial and administrative independence, with its members meeting four times a year.

The basic framework for the governance of the state is decided by the Majlis Oman as a whole. The Basic Statute of State also defines the roles and obligatory responsibilities of all Omani citizens. The legal system of Oman is based on the Ibadhi interpretation of Shari'a law (Islamic law), as well as tribal custom and traditions.

Oman is divided into nine regions for administrative purposes. Four of these areas are called governorates, and the remaining five are called regions, with Muscat, the capital, acting as the center for government. The governorates are Muscat, Dhofar, Musandam, and Al Buraimi, and the regions are Al Batinah, Al Dakhiliyah, Al Sharqiyah, Al Dhahira, and Al Wusta.

Each governorate or region is subdivided into *wilayats*, and finally into *niyabats*. Each *wilayat* is overseen by a government-appointed *wali*. A *wali's* role is predominately local, unless he is part of one of the Councils. A *wali* acts out of his office and settles minor disputes, collects taxes for his *wilayat*, and generally sees that peace is maintained in his district. *Walis* fall under the Ministry of Interior with the exception of the *Wali* of Dhofar, who holds a position in the Cabinet and has more far-reaching powers.

FOREIGN RELATIONS

Oman is on friendly terms with many foreign countries. The Omani government's foreign policy includes maintaining good relations with its immediate neighbors, upholding its maritime traditions, and  encouraging positive, peaceful solutions toward conflict. Oman is one of the founding members of the Gulf Cooperation Council (GCC), a member of the United Nations, and a member of the Arab League. In terms of free trade, Oman encourages private and public sectors in addition to encouraging the expansion of international agreements.

THE ECONOMY

Oman's economy has been largely shaped by its maritime trade and the sudden, unexpected discovery of oil in 1964. Today oil and gas, agricultural exports—mainly dates and limes—animals and animal products, fishing, mining, and, to a lesser extent, traditional handicrafts make up Oman's economy. The country's strategic location coupled with its political stability are important points in its favor. With the modernization of its ports in recent years, Oman is repositioning itself for long-term growth.

Industry

While its oil finds were not as extensive as those of the neighboring GCC countries, Oman has seen a steady flow of income from its oil reserves, especially when oil prices reached record levels in recent years. The oil and gas industry currently contributes 84 percent of the country's global exports.

In addition to the petrochemical industry, Oman has a long tradition of boatbuilding. Traditional craft are still built today using local materials and methods that have been passed down through the generations. More modern methods of shipbuilding have been introduced in the larger cities, as more and more boats are required for the modern ports. Other major industries are copper mining, manufacturing of nonmetallic mineral products, chemicals, and chemical products.

Agriculture

Oman has a long tradition of farming, and the southern coast is lined with date and lime plantations. The Omani lime is appreciated throughout the GCC and is exported to countries such as the UAE, Bahrain, and Saudi Arabia, where it is used in local cuisine. Dates, an important ingredient of the Arab way of life, are always found in an Arab home, and Omani dates are considered to be among the finest. The date palm itself is a useful and versatile plant: the fronds are used in basket weaving, and for making *barasti* (a fairly thin woven material used for huts), *karijins* (a more substantial

material also used in hut building), mats, and food containers.

Other crops include melons, bananas, and alfalfa. Approximately 1 percent of the country is under cultivation today.

With more than 1,200 miles (2,000 km) of coastline and around 130 species of fish and shellfish, fishing still makes an important contribution to life in Oman. Commercial-scale fishing accounts for more than 100,000 tons of fish caught per year.

Tourism

Tourism did not play a large role in the economy of Oman until recent years, but now the country has opened its doors to more foreign nationals by making its easier to obtain an entry visa, and by building many new hotels. Using Oman's already bountiful natural attractions, ecotourism is one further aspect that has made the country increasingly popular. Annual festivals and events that highlight the true values and traditions of Oman have seen a steady increase in the number of visitors, particularly from the other GCC countries nearby. The cooler climates of Salalah during the long summer holidays in the Middle East are a further draw, and the stable, safe, tranquil nature of Oman attracts more and more visitors, who then want to come again to explore more of the country.

chapter two

VALUES & ATTITUDES

Oman is well-known for its friendly people and peaceful setting. Omanis are very considerate of other people, and will generally do all they can to ensure good social relations. They are welcoming, and understand the importance of foreign visitors and workers in their country; however, they have high standards and expect their local rules to be embraced and upheld.

Religion, family, and personal honor are among the most important aspects of life for an Omani, who will go out of his way to ensure that he acts in an honorable fashion, and that his family is treated in the same way. There is very much an attitude that if these values are maintained and cherished, everything else will fall into place.

While Oman has not enjoyed the same quick prosperity as its neighboring GCC countries, the pace of development has been steady and well planned, with revenues from the petrochemical industry put to good use. Omani traditions, whether social or religious, have been carefully maintained and are apparent in daily life throughout the country, and people in rural areas are encouraged to keep up their traditional crafts and skills.

With the opening of more higher education facilities and the modernization of existing ones, young Omanis are equipped to make a useful contribution to their society. Most find gainful employment once their studies have been completed, in contrast with those in neighboring countries.

Oman society is a relationship-based one, as we have seen, with people coming before time. What Omanis lack in timekeeping is made up for in sincerity. A handshake is binding, and while it may seem that arrangements are easily cancelled, promises are not so easily forgotten. A cancelled appointment does not mean the end of a working relationship, and it will be rescheduled. It is important to be patient and understanding of the Omani attitude toward time (see page 70).

STATUS AND SOCIAL STRUCTURE

Despite recent economic and social changes in Oman, the country still remains a tribal one. A family name continues to be an important identifier, in terms of both wealth and social importance. Heads of the Omani tribes are able to consult with the Sultan on important political issues, which has kept these leaders in their traditional roles and continues to assist in maintaining a peaceful, stable country. The discovery of oil in the 1960s certainly created internal social change as the revenues began to come in. Oman has shown its ability for forethought once more with a social welfare system in place that includes pensions for Omanis once they reach retirement age, as well as disability benefits. Oman has placed an increasingly important focus on building its own national workforce. This includes the current Omanization program that exists and is implemented in companies across the country. Status within the country comes not only from material wealth and possessions but also from social and political connections.

Middle-class Omani families are generally working professionals who live in an urban environment. They may adopt Western dress for part of the time, but revert to their national dress for important events and attending the mosque. Upward mobility is a likely possibility for these Omanis. The lower classes of society are considered to be those living in a rural environment who have limited access to modern amenities and social change. They tend to be engaged in traditional agricultural activities. There is also a segment of Omani society that is extremely wealthy; as with the middle class, they may have adopted a more Western style of dress. It is more common, however, for the men to wear a *dishdasha* (an ankle-length robe, usually white, with long sleeves) while they drive their imported German cars to business meetings.

Omani women continue to face challenges in their attempt to cross over from their mainly family-oriented, home-based role to the working environment. While more women are working in sectors such as finance, medicine, and government, these tend to be women who have been brought up in urban areas with the opportunity to attend a local university. Women in rural areas continue to stay within the home, with little chance of being able to change their personal position.

RELIGION

Islam is the official religion of Oman; people of other religions are free to practice in their own places of worship. The majority of Omanis are Ibadhis, with a much smaller minority being Shi'a. Ibadhism, named after its founder, the scholar and writer Jabir Bin Zaid Al 'Azdi (642–714), is known as a moderate and conservative sect of Islam.

There are six basic beliefs in Islam, called the Articles of Faith: faith in the unity of God, faith in angels, faith in prophets, faith in books of revelation, faith in an afterlife, and faith in destiny. There are five pillars of Islam: *shahadah* (profession of faith), *salat* (prayer), *zakat* (payment of alms), *sawm* (fasting during the holy month of Ramadan), and *hajj* (pilgrimage to Holy Mecca). These are considered the duty of each and every Muslim.

Islam is more than just a religion: it is a way of life, with the Koran (*Qur'an*) providing precise instructions on how to live one's life while being mindful of religion and Allah. Muslims believe that the Koran, which is made up of 114 *sura*s (chapters), is the actual word of God, as revealed to the Prophet Mohammed by the Angel Gabriel. There is a second source, called the *Hadith*, the sayings and teachings of the Prophet Mohammed.

Muslims are forbidden to eat pork and drink alcohol; but, as with every religion, some break these stipulations. Muslims believe that their lives are left up to the will of God, and have a strong faith in fate. There are no atheist or agnostic Omanis, and it is considered highly immoral to declare anything other than a belief in God.

The Koran itself is highly visible throughout the country, with copies in the home and workplaces, and quotations from it are found engraved on buildings, and on plaques hanging from walls and over doors. When not in use, the Koran is stored closed in a clean, dry place, nothing is ever placed on top of it, and it is never put on the floor. A wooden holder is often used to prop the Koran open when it is being read while sitting on the floor. The Koran can be found for sale in certain outlets throughout the country, with translations in many different languages; visitors may even be presented with a copy by an Omani. However, proper respect for the Koran is extremely important, and mishandling can cause great offense. Non-Muslims should hold the Koran with some sort of barrier between it and their hands, such as a piece of clean cloth or a glove. It is also important to ensure that your hands are clean underneath the cloth.

As with all Muslims, Omanis are expected to pray five times a day, whether in their own homes, in their work environment, or in a mosque. In the workplace there is usually a room set aside for prayers. The call to prayer resonates throughout the country from the smallest rural mosque to the huge Sultan Qaboos Grand Mosque in Muscat. Men and women do not generally pray together in public, and there are separate rooms for women in mosques. In the home, women pray behind the men, although it is more common for prayers to be said alone in a quiet area. Prayer times are issued in local daily papers, in Arabic and English. The direction of Mecca is marked in hotel rooms as a guide for visiting Muslims wishing to pray in the privacy of their rooms.

Muslims are required to donate a portion of their annual earnings to the poor and to charity, as long as these earnings are above a certain threshold. The different sects of Islam have different requirements, although the end result is the same—that the wealthy share some of their good fortune with those less fortunate. Further donations can be made at any time, and these are considered to attain a divine reward.

NATIONAL PRIDE

The Omani people love their ruler, and have no qualms about displaying their affection as often and as notably as possible. Some of the biggest celebrations in the country occur on Sultan Qaboos's Birthday and National Day, and Renaissance Day, with all Omanis joining in with the festivities in some way. Omanis generally do not discuss their country in a negative way, regardless of their own opinions, preferring to share their knowledge of all that it has to offer. Oman enjoys a rich heritage and history, as well as natural beauty, and Omanis are only too pleased to go into detail about its progress and accomplishments, especially under the rule of Sultan Qaboos.

There is a strong personal pride in the national dress, with Omani men wearing the traditional white *dishdasha* on a daily basis as well as their elaborately decorated *khunjars* (daggers).

PERSONAL HONOR

In Omani society, upholding one's personal honor and reputation is of extreme importance.

Bringing shame to a family name is unforgivable, and is to be avoided at all costs. Family tradition remains firmly in the Omani mind-set and restricts both actions and words that would cause shame. The tribal family system that remains in place in modern Oman ensures that strong family bonds exist. Families often live in the same area, if not the same village, so an individual must maintain his own good reputation in order that his entire family will keep theirs.

ATTITUDES TO WOMEN

While the rural areas of Oman may still be lacking in suitable further education and business placements, the women who are brought up in the larger cities are benefiting from the Sultan's and the government's forward-thinking attitude toward women in the workplace and women in the home. Girls are ensured the same level of education as boys, and university places are available for female students.

Once their studies are complete, Omani women are encouraged to go into business, whether working for an existing company or on their own account. Women are considered of great importance in Omani culture, and their roles as wives and mothers are highly respected, even if they have a job outside the home and rely on domestic help. Women have been able to campaign for places in the Majlis ash-Shura since 1994. More recently women have been appointed to government positions; these include Dr. Rajiha Bint Abdulamir Bin Ali, Minister of Tourism, and Dr. Sharifa Bint Khalfan Al Yahya'eyah, Minister of Social Development.

Outside the cities, women tend to remain in the more traditional role of wife and mother, and are generally expected to stay in the home. Schooling ends far earlier for all children in these areas as the financial burdens of the family are placed upon their shoulders.

Regardless of geographical location, women are still expected to retain the family honor by remaining virgins until they are married, and to behave in a manner that fits in with their family traditions. Omani families are still stricter when it comes to monitoring the behavior and actions of girls when compared with boys.

The role of wife and mother is still very much predetermined by local tradition. A woman is expected to be married. The Koran details the laws regarding her dowry, what will happen if there is a divorce, and her inheritance if her husband dies. Polygamy is permitted in Islam, and thus in Oman, allowing a man to have up to four wives. While multiple marriages do still occur, financial constraints usually mean that a man will take no more than two wives. A second marriage often occurs when fertility problems arise, although the advances and availability of modern medicine mean this is happening less frequently. The first wife is held in higher regard than later wives, and a man must be able to treat each wife in exactly the same way in order to have more than one.

Women in rural areas, especially those of older generations, continue to wear a full face mask

made from stiff fabric, while younger women opt for the lighter *shayla* (head scarf), which still covers the hair and preserves a woman's modesty but is less restrictive than the mask. The majority of women wear the *abaya* (a thin, ankle-length robe, usually black, that fastens in front), although more and more are opting for modest Western clothing with a *shayla* in the cities and while at work. There are many more colorful and elaborately embroidered traditional women's costumes, with different colors and designs coming from the different regions of Oman. However, these beautiful garments are now mainly reserved for special occasions.

WORK ETHIC

Omanis in general want to learn, work hard, and contribute to their society. However, it would appear that the younger segment of the workforce is not used to the hard work of their ancestors and is finding it more difficult to settle into long-term jobs. While official unemployment figures are low, it seems that finding gainful, lasting employment is harder in the cities and more urban areas than the rural ones. In the rural areas, where agriculture in often a family's only livelihood, children are involved in the family business from as young as possible so that they can take over from their older male relatives. Tribal bonds mean that a single person does not usually leave the area of his birth; however whole families have been known to move into the cities to seek employment. Religion plays a strong role within the mind-set of all Muslims: the Koran teaches that a person has responsibility toward his family—not only his own wife and children, but his parents and sisters as well—and that he should go out to work to provide them with their basic requirements. Family is important, and it is not uncommon for an Omani to cancel a planned meeting in order to attend to family matters.

With an Omanization program firmly in place throughout Oman, companies are required to hire a minimum number of Omani nationals for their workforce, the actual number being decided according to certain criteria and determined by the appropriate ministry. The aim is to utilize Oman's own workforce before bringing in more foreign nationals. Oman has a detailed labor law that protects the rights and entitlements of both Omani nationals and foreign workers in the country.

TIME MANAGEMENT

Many Westerners find the Omani attitude to time frustrating. In Oman time is not money, and takes second place to personal relationships. One of the most important words in the Arabic language is "*Insha'allah*" (God willing); it is used frequently by Arabs throughout the world, usually in response to statements such as "See you tomorrow," or "I'm going away next week." It is also used in business settings when discussing anything to do with time and the future, for example an upcoming journey, or the delivery of goods. Omanis believe that everything is in the hands of God, and only He will determine the outcome; to omit the "*Insha'allah*" would be to tempt fate. The word is also used to answer questions, and can be quite noncommittal, so perhaps the answer is a yes, a no, or a maybe. It can be quite trying to foreigners!

As Omani daily life is built around prayer times, meetings can be delayed while prayers are performed. Sole proprietors sometimes close their shops or other businesses completely while they attend to their prayers, either at the local mosque or in a private place, returning after twenty minutes or so. There is some flexibility in the work or school environment as to when prayers are performed as long as they are completed.

Appointments and engagements are therefore treated rather more loosely than in the West. Your may well find that arrangements are cancelled at the last minute—and perhaps only at the time you expected them to take place.

chapter three

CUSTOMS &

TRADITIONS

The Islamic calendar is based on the lunar cycle,
which means that most annual festivals and public
holidays are observed on different dates each year,
and may be announced only a few days beforehand
in the local media. The exceptions are National Day
and Sultan Qaboos's Birthday, and New Year's Day
(in the Gregorian calendar). The start of Ramadan
is often known only the night before, and most
Omanis will watch public television stations to
hear the announcement, as they will begin to fast
from sunrise the following morning.

RELIGIOUS FESTIVALS AND HOLIDAYS
Ramadan
The ninth month of the Islamic calendar,
Ramadan, is the most holy month of the year. For
this month, a minimum of twenty-eight days,
Muslims are required to fast, refraining from
eating, drinking, smoking, and sexual relations,
from sunrise to sunset. They are required to

behave with special moderation and show extra kindness toward others. It is also a time for reflection, reading the Koran, and learning more about Islam.

The sighting of the new moon, a thin crescent that appears at the beginning of the new lunar month, heralds the start of Ramadan. Modern innovations mean that the first day of Ramadan can be predicted, and Oman has upheld the tradition of using the skills of the Moonsighting Committee. The date of Ramadan advances by approximately ten days each year, due to the lunar nature of the Islamic calendar.

Ramadan is a time of restraint, and fasting can be very hard to do, especially during the summer months when the days can be twelve or thirteen hours long and the heat still rages. The first few days are usually the most difficult as people settle into their routines of observing the rules, and perhaps arriving at work slightly later in the mornings. Patience can be in short supply and, understandably, tempers can be lost. The late nights spent eating and drinking can also take a toll, often resulting in tiredness and loss of concentration. However, once the first week is over people seem to settle down and take these restrictions in stride.

Business and school hours are reduced throughout the country, and most people retire to their homes at noon to pray and rest. There is a

flurry of activity in the late afternoon as the preparations begin for *iftar*, the breaking of the fast. The roads can get very busy with people rushing home to break their fast, resulting in impatient drivers—regardless of their religion—and frustrating traffic jams. Parking outside a mosque can be tricky, as cars are left every which way, hazard lights flashing, while the drivers hurry in to perform their prayers. Many people break their fast with some dates and water before attending the mosque for prayers. Outside mosques, huge plastic tablecloths are laid along the ground and any Muslims who have been fasting and find themselves far from home, or unable to afford a proper meal, are offered free food. These meals are funded by *zakat* (alms) given by local benefactors or collected during the year.

Families and friends spend the evening together once they have completed their prayers. The meal is a huge spread of soup, several rice and meat dishes, salads, vegetables, plenty of tea, and sweets afterward. It can last for several hours, and the gathering often goes on into the early hours of the morning. This is a month for visiting, for sharing the bounty that most can afford, and for goodwill to neighbors and fellow countrymen.

You should be warned that, though non-Muslim visitors to the country are not expected to fast, eating or drinking in public is forbidden throughout Oman during Ramadan; the consequences for doing so are severe. Most restaurants, fast-food outlets, and smaller shops will be closed until after *iftar* prayers at sunset. Allowances are made for tourists visiting the country during this month, as some hotel restaurants will be screened off and serve food. Alcohol is forbidden until after sunset, bars and nightclubs in hotels will remain closed throughout the day, and even then the consumption of alcohol is limited to in-house guests only.

Dress should be conservative during this time, especially for women, who should remember the rules about covering their shoulders and the tops of their arms, and should wear skirts that come well below the knee, or trousers. There is no need for visiting women to cover their hair in public. The rules are slightly more relaxed for men, long shorts or trousers with a T-shirt or shirt being perfectly acceptable.

Eid al-Fitr
Eid al-Fitr marks the end of the holy month of Ramadan. It is usually a three-day public holiday, but this depends on whether the holiday falls midweek or on the weekend. It is a time of celebration and feasting, with families gathering together to enjoy good food. People greet each other with the traditional "*Eid Mubarak*," and there is a general sense of goodwill and merriment throughout the country. The prayers on the first day of Eid are very important and, if possible, Omanis head to the mosque to perform their prayers. During the last few days of Ramadan, people go shopping to buy new clothes to wear during Eid; children usually get a new outfit as well as small gifts of sweets and money.

Eid al-Adha

Eid al-Adha is an even bigger celebration, with most businesses and government offices closed for three days. This holiday marks the end of Hajj (the pilgrimage to Mecca), and is considered one of the most important events in the Islamic calendar. If possible, families slaughter livestock, generally a goat, and offer the meat to the poor. The first and second days are generally spent visiting family and close friends while enjoying food treats such as the traditional Omani *halwa* and *arsia*, a delicious meal of lamb and rice.

Islamic New Year

The Islamic calendar starts with Muharram, the first month of the year. Ras as-Sana, the first day of the New Year, is marked with a public holiday. Although Government, schools, and businesses are closed for one day, there are no specific public celebrations.

Mouloud

Mouloud, the Prophet Mohammed's Birthday, is marked with a public holiday in both private and public sectors. If the holiday falls on a weekend, a weekday public holiday is usually announced. There are some small local celebrations, such as a special song, "*Al Mawlid*," which is performed in the Musandam region.

Leilat al-Meiraj

Leilat al-Meiraj, the Ascension of the Prophet, is also marked by a one-day public holiday. There are no special celebrations. However, Muslims celebrate the spiritual night journey of the Prophet by reading the Koran and performing extra prayers in addition to their other five daily prayers.

OTHER PUBLIC HOLIDAYS
New Year's Day

January 1 is a public holiday. Some venues may have fireworks and private celebrations the evening before. New Year's Day itself is a time for family gatherings and visiting, as are most public holidays in Oman. You will see families gathered at the roadside for impromptu picnics and barbecues.

National Day and H. M. Sultan Qaboos's Birthday

Omani National Day is celebrated annually on November 18, which is also Sultan Qaboos's birthday. It is a public holiday and a day of immense pride and joy for the Omani people. The highlight of the day is a military parade of various branches of the armed forces, which takes place at

different venues over the years, personally selected by the Sultan. Throughout the country, the excitement of the day is reflected in the colorful bunting that hangs along the main roads and the Omani flags that fly from every possible mast as well as the huge, regal portraits of the Sultan that are erected. Buildings in the cities are draped with garlands of colored lights, making the city shimmer and shine by night. The festivities also include camel races and traditional dancing, and of course, as on most Omani holidays, a vast array of local cuisine. The culmination of this exciting holiday is a dazzling display of fireworks.

Renaissance Day
In 2006 Sultan Qaboos issued a royal decree stating that July 23 would be marked as a public

holiday, to be called Renaissance Day. It celebrates his accession to the throne and the launch of a new era in Oman's history.

Mother's Day

While technically not a public holiday, Mother's Day is celebrated on the second Sunday in May, with children giving flowers, cards, and other small gifts to their mothers. There are usually displays throughout retail outlets in Oman announcing the actual date.

WEDDINGS

As with most societies, in Oman a wedding is an occasion for joy and celebration. It is one of the most important events in an Omani's life, and in the life of his or her parents. The bride and groom will have been introduced by other family members, and may have met several times, but only in the presence of chaperones from their respective families. They will spend no time together unsupervised until they are married. Both bride and groom must be over the age of eighteen when they marry.

The family is very important in Omani life, and the in-laws interact with each other frequently at family events and social gatherings. The newly married couple may live with the groom's parents for some time, so it is considered vital that everyone is able to get along; many marriages take place between families that have known each other a considerable length of time.

Wedding Decorations

A few days before the ceremony the bride will have her hands, forearms, and feet elaborately and intricately adorned with henna, a reddish pigment that dyes the skin. These beautiful patterned decorations last for several weeks.

As with so many aspects of a Muslim's life, the Koran details how the marriage contract will be carried out, and sets out how much dowry (*mahr*) is to be paid by the groom to his bride's family. This dowry is usually money—but may be, or may include, jewelry and gold—and is considered an indication of how prepared a man is to fulfill his marital responsibilities. It is usually given to the bride by her parents so that she leaves the family home with a financial cushion; it can be useful if her husband dies or if there is a divorce. Once the dowry has been settled, a legal or religious representative oversees the signing of the contract and the marriage ceremony, with usually only the groom, the bride's father, and other male relatives in attendance. Two male witnesses must be present. Once the groom and his new father-in-law have joined hands the contract is complete.

The wedding celebration is a huge affair—as elaborate as can be afforded—with music, entertainment, and lavish quantities of food, and possibly lasting three days. These festivities come with a large financial burden, borne usually by the groom's parents, but frequently by the groom himself. Wedding celebrations are often very public affairs, with wedding tents set up in the street and the groom and his attendants dancing and singing in traditional Omani fashion. The groom and his male relatives and friends celebrate separately from the bride and her family and friends. The men wear immaculate white *dishdasha*, and often carry their traditional *khunjars* and rifles during the celebrations. The bride and the women will remain indoors, perhaps nearby or at her parents' home.

On the last night of the celebrations, the bride and groom finally come together in front of their families and friends. They will usually leave the following day on their honeymoon.

FOLKWAYS

Jinn, or genies, feature strongly in Arabic folklore.
They are mentioned in the Koran, and are said to
be invisible, supernatural beings that have free
will and are capable of being either good or evil.
They are said to be able to whisper to one's soul,
and it is believed that an evil *jinn* can turn a
person toward evil.

The concept of the "Evil Eye" is well-known
throughout the Middle East. Omanis believe very
strongly in its power. The Evil Eye comes from
other people's jealousy of beauty, money, power,
and material possessions. Stories abound of
situations such as having one's new watch
admired and then the following day the strap
breaking and the watch being lost. To protect
themselves from the Evil Eye, Omanis say
certain prayers and read selected *sura*
from the Koran. Women and children
also wear black *kohl* around their eyes.
The most common, highly visible way to
ward off the harmful thoughts of others is
with the blue glass "salty eyes" that appear on all
kinds of accessories, such as key rings, bracelets,
and pendants.

chapter four

MAKING FRIENDS

Friendship is an important part of Omani society, and Omanis are well-known for their warm and hospitable attitude, both toward their own people and toward visitors to their country. While the relationships between men and women in Oman are carefully segregated, friendships with foreigners are more relaxed. Omani men are more likely to make friends with foreign males, but they may befriend foreign women too; Omani women will normally befriend only other females. Friends get together as often as daily life and work allow. They trust and care for each other, and act in each other's best interests.

New friends may be made through business or work, through a common interest, or by an introduction from a family member. Generosity and hospitality are ingrained into Omani culture, and are the driving force behind most actions. It is common for virtual strangers to be invited to an Omani's home to eat, and perhaps to meet his children. Travelers will always be invited into homes along the way, even the most humble of huts, for a cool drink and some dates.

ATTITUDES TO FOREIGNERS

Oman initially encouraged foreigners into their country for economic reasons, to work in the sectors where Omanis lacked the necessary skills to perform certain jobs. In the early days of Sultan Qaboos's rule the number of tourists permitted to enter the country was closely controlled, and visas were hard to come by. Recently, Oman has changed its policies and has welcomed more and more tourists into the country each year, understanding the importance of a healthy tourism sector to their economic situation. As long as visitors to Oman respect its traditional values and culture, the people of Oman will welcome them. Omanis are proud of their country and their history, and are more than willing to share information about their surroundings with interested foreigners, and talk about their roots.

These foreigners are a source of interest for Omanis, too. People living in the towns are used to seeing tourists wandering their streets and shopping in the *souq*, but it can be harder for rural Omanis to adjust to their appearance. Children living in country areas run out of their homes to inspect strangers—usually hoping that some sort of treat will be forthcoming. It is important to remember that while many wealthy Omanis are well educated, and may have completed some of their schooling abroad as well as working there before returning home to Oman, the absolute reverse is true for the poorer people. They have had no exposure to any form of Western society, which is very different from their own.

Omanis don't date in the way that Westerners do. As we have seen, they usually meet their intended spouse through family members and are closely chaperoned until they are married. However, Omani men are able to marry foreign women, and therefore dating can happen. These relationships tend to be kept very discreet until the couple becomes engaged or marries, so as not to cause offense. An Omani woman is not permitted to marry a foreigner unless he is from one of the GCC countries.

GREETINGS

When you meet people it is important to greet them appropriately, whether it is in the street or at a planned meeting. Warmth and friendliness are essential when issuing these greetings, and your delivery may affect an Omani's opinion of you, as first impressions are very important. It is considered rude to see someone you know, whether a friend or even just an acquaintance, and not offer some form of greeting. A wave is considered dismissive, and does not suffice as a greeting.

Women will kiss each other on both cheeks. If they know each other well, they may give more than the two kisses. Men may shake hands if they are unfamiliar with each other, and a closer relationship warrants a warm pat on the back. Close male friends and relatives may give each other a kiss on each cheek. People of opposite sexes do not shake hands or offer any other form of physical greeting, especially when they do not know each other. A man should never offer his hand to a woman: he should wait and see what she does first. It is common for younger people to kiss their older relatives on the head as an expression of respect and love.

One of the most complicated issues surrounding meeting people in Oman is which spoken greeting to use. The most common form is "*Al salaam a'alaykum*" ("Peace be upon you"), the correct reply to which is "*A'alaykum salaam*" ("And peace be upon you"). When a person enters a room, he will offer this greeting generally, and everyone in the room will reply, whether they know him or not. It is considered rude not to respond.

The greeting offered in the morning is "*Sabah al khair*" ("Good morning"). The correct reply is "*Sabah al noor.*" In the afternoon and evening, the greeting is "*Masah al khair,*" and the response is "*Masah al noor.*" "*Marhabbah*" (Hello) is used between good friends.

DRESS

It is important to dress with care and consideration in Oman. Omanis are very conservative, and tend to be immaculately turned out themselves. Visitors should dress for the situations they are likely to encounter. Friday is an important day in the Middle East, as it is a holy day and the day of rest, and this should be remembered when dressing to go out on a Friday.

Women should wear loose, modest clothing, ensuring that their upper arms and shoulders are covered. Skirts or trousers should be long, with the legs covered to below the knee. Absolutely no tight, revealing clothing should worn in public at any time. A light shawl should be carried for situations where extra coverage is required, for example in the rural villages. Footwear should be comfortable. Men should as a general rule wear trousers with a shirt or T-shirt. In the city today, long shorts are acceptable for men as long as they are below the knee. Sandals are fine for most of the time, but note that some hotels do not allow them in their restaurants. Be aware that a woman can be fined or even deported for being improperly dressed. Even men should note that wearing shorts in the mountains on a Friday, the religious day, can result in being banned from a village.

Town dwellers are naturally more modern than country people and tend to be more accepting of foreigners and their modes of dress. Take extra care when deciding what to wear when going out of town, and cover up more. What may be acceptable in the cities is not appropriate in the villages, and some Western clothes can cause offense in rural areas.

The heat that lasts for most of the year is an important factor. Loose cotton clothing that covers you up is not only cooler than other materials but will also help to protect you from sunburn.

People in Oman tend to stare, especially at women, regardless of what they wear, but visitors will attract less attention if they are wearing moderate clothing.

INVITATIONS HOME

Omanis are quick to invite you to their home
even if you have only just been introduced,

because they are
proud of their
homes and enjoy
sharing food
with their
friends and
relatives. It is
considered
courteous
to accept any
such invitation,
where the
gathering is
likely to include,
apart from your host, his children, possibly his
wife, and other relatives and friends.

An Omani's wife will go out of her way to
provide an elaborate spread for a guest to her
home. There may well be domestic help, but your
host will be proud to show off his wife's cooking.

It is important to take a gift with you on your
visit, and not arrive empty-handed. Chocolates,
nuts, and dates are always very well received,
preferably in an elegant box or otherwise
attractively displayed. There are roasteries—small

shops selling chocolates and all varieties of nuts, as well as coffee—in all the cities, which sell these gifts elaborately packaged and ready to present, or you can select your own contents. Your gift does not have to be the largest arrangement in the shop. Bear in mind that Omanis have many guests coming through their homes, and these items will be shared with them. Dates are sold in supermarkets as well as specialist shops and make a perfect, useful present. Don't give flowers—unlike in Western cultures, they are usually given only between women, and on occasions such as birthdays and the birth of a child, rather than when visiting for a meal. Your hostess might not even own a vase in which to put them.

HOSPITALITY

The hospitable Omanis usually have a room in their home, called a *majlis*, specifically for entertaining. Some larger homes have two, one being for the men and his guests and the second for his wife to entertain her female friends and family, but it is more usual for the woman to receive her visitors in the family areas of the house.

The guest is of extreme importance in Omani culture, and no effort will be spared to ensure that you are comfortable and enjoy your time with the family. You will be offered a choice of fruit juice, coffee, or water, as well as fruits, dates, and small cookies. Refusal of food or drink in an Omani home will be met with confusion and offers of a greater selection in an attempt to find something to your taste. It is best to accept a drink and something to eat even if you're not hungry or thirsty, in order to appease your host and, more importantly, his wife, who will be fussing behind the scenes even if you don't meet her during your visit. There is no such thing as short notice when visiting in Oman—there will always be something ready to offer guests.

Omanis will insist on paying for dinner when in a restaurant, and friendly tussles can occur over the bill, with everyone trying to pay. The "winner" will often say that the "loser" can pick up the bill next time!

TABOO SUBJECTS

There are a number of taboo subjects in Omani culture, and most are associated with Islam. Discussions involving Islam in a negative way will not be tolerated by the majority of Omanis, and certainly should not be brought up while visiting an Omani's house as a guest. Religion itself is not a taboo subject, and any Omani would be more than happy to explain any aspect of his religion to a foreigner. However, if the subject of religion comes up, you may be asked about your own beliefs. You will be expected to have a religion. The idea of atheism is not something that is well-known in Omani culture. Attempting to explain this may be met with confusion and even more questions than you are able to answer, so it is best avoided.

Pork is forbidden to Muslims—they may not eat it, prepare it, or serve it. It is a subject that is not open for discussion, and should be avoided, unless it is to issue a warning to a person about to eat some unknowingly. While alcohol is not strictly a taboo subject, Muslims are not permitted to drink or serve it, so it is best to avoid the topic entirely.

Politics is discussed in Omani society, especially around the time of the elections for Majlis ash-Shura, but it is not appropriate to discuss the monarchy in a negative way, as it is highly respected throughout the country. It would be considered very offensive to do so.

Homosexuality is illegal in Oman and should not be discussed at all. To bring the topic up in any social situation involving Omanis would be deeply offensive; in fact, sexuality in any form is not openly discussed.

A man should never ask an Omani man to whom he is not related about his wife, as this is considered rude. (It is, however, acceptable for a woman to ask after the wife of an Omani man.) If you have to find a subject to continue the small talk, you can ask about his health and that of his children, but domestic matters are considered to be private and are not usually discussed outside the immediate family environment. Omanis don't generally talk about matters such as how much money they make.

Sticking to safe topics is the best way to keep a conversation going. Omanis enjoy talking about their country, their fellow Omanis, and their Sultan. They also enjoy learning more about their friends, so it is perfectly acceptable for you to talk about yourself, your home, and your family. If you become involved in a conversation that you find uncomfortable, it is perfectly acceptable to change the subject. You can attempt to explain, gently but firmly, that this is not something that you wish to discuss any further, and move on.

chapter five

PRIVATE & FAMILY LIFE

People in the cities and urban areas of Oman live in modern villas or apartment blocks. Urban homes are mainly built from brick and cement and tend to have a flat roof. Most have a *majlis* (meeting room) lined with cushions for guests, with carpets or rugs on the floor, and low coffee tables for drinks and snacks. Modern Omanis may have sofas and armchairs around the room, rather than the traditional cushions.

Rural houses are built of mud or brick and often have *barasti* (woven palm frond) coverings

on the roof. These homes have very shallow foundations, or are simply built on the ground. Houses near the shoreline and in the mountainous areas are often built of stone. Most Omani homes are built around a central courtyard, which is used for a variety of purposes.

The Omani home is a busy one, with family coming and going all day long. Omanis enjoy the hustle and bustle of family life, and an extra person at the dinner table doesn't faze the female family members in the least.

THE HOUSEHOLD AND FAMILY

The Omani home is based on the nuclear family, and often has members of the extended family also living with them, but very rarely includes unrelated people unless they are short-term guests. Many young Omanis marry and remain in the groom's parents' house while they are saving to build a home of their own. Elderly parents generally move in with their children once they are unable to look after themselves. Individuals do not live alone as a general rule, preferring to stay within their family environment.

Omani home life is very traditional. The father is the head of the household. He is usually the main breadwinner, he makes the rules, and his authority is rarely questioned by any member of his family. The wife and mother is in charge of household management, including organizing and supervising the domestic help—most households have at least one maid, probably from India, Sri Lanka, the Philippines, or Indonesia, to assist with cleaning, cooking, and child care. The wife's financial needs are met by her husband, unless she goes out to work herself—something that is becoming more common in modern urban Oman. If the wife has a job, she will still be required to oversee all the household work, for maintaining a clean, well-run home is essential to an Omani woman, and food must be prepared regardless of other activities that may impinge on her time.

The eldest son usually takes over from his father as head of the family if his father dies or becomes unable to manage because of illness or age. This son will then be responsible for his mother and any younger siblings until they marry and leave the family home, as well as the running of the family home.

Omani families tend to be large. It is rare to find an Omani family with only one child or none; in fact a man may well take a second wife if his first is unable to bear him a child. Children are believed to be gifts from God, and are seen as a blessing and a pleasure. They are welcomed and fussed over at family gatherings.

It is unusual for parents to go out together and leave their children at home—unless the occasion is particularly formal, or work related—and it is common to see entire families out after dark. Children are often allowed to stay up late in the evenings, especially if they have had a rest in the afternoon. During Ramadan, children enjoy eating and drinking until the same time as the adults, even if they are not fasting during the day.

Children are welcome in most places in Oman, and are taken out to restaurants, shops, and to visit friends at all times of the day and night. Women tend to be very affectionate toward all children, pinching cheeks, patting hands, and giving kisses even to children they don't know.

Growing Up in Oman

As in the neighboring Gulf countries, Omani children start school at the age of three and in the urban areas continue their studies until they are eighteen. It is common for boys in the rural areas to leave school early to help with the family business, whether it is farming, fishing, or another agricultural activity.

The school day starts early, with classes beginning before 8:00 a.m. to try to avoid the heat of the day. There is usually a break in the morning for a snack and for the children to play outside,

and a further break later on. The school day ends
at 1:00 p.m. for very young children, and between
2:00 p.m. and 3:00 p.m. for older ones. Once
home, children will eat their lunch with their
mother. The meal may be prepared and served by
the mother or by the domestic helper.
Children often take a rest after lunch
before tackling their homework. It is
common for middle- and upper-class
Omani households to hire a tutor to
assist their children with their
homework after school and to provide
extra lessons in the more difficult
subjects as needed, and particularly for
classical Arabic and Islamic studies.

There is little time during the school day for extra tuition, so this has to be taken care of at home.

Omani boys enjoy football (soccer), and can often be seen out dressed in bright, local team colors, and kicking a ball around. The girls generally remain indoors after school, helping their mothers with the preparations for the evening meal and other household chores, and studying or reading from the Koran.

After leaving school young people, depending on their family's situation, either look for gainful employment or continue their education in one of Oman's universities. Further education is an aspiration for many Omanis. There are a limited number of places available, and competition is fierce. Many school graduates must take a job that offers training. The lucky few are able to secure jobs with opportunities for further study abroad. Some middle- and upper-class Omanis elect to study abroad, with the United Kingdom and America being popular choices.

Teenage boys in the cities can often be found hanging out at the local malls and shopping centers, and in coffee shops, cinemas, and entertainment centers. The coffee shops usually offer *shisha*, or hubbly bubbly (Arabic water pipe), to their customers. Smoking *shisha* is illegal for anyone under eighteen; however, underage smoking does happen, as it is seen as a fashionable and grown-up thing to do. The legal age for obtaining a driver's license is eighteen, and most young male Omanis jump at the chance to be mobile as soon as they can. Teenage girls have far stricter boundaries restricting what they can do and where they are allowed to go. They will often go shopping or have a meal in a group, perhaps with an older female family member as a chaperone, who will remain with them or nearby. Parents keep in close contact with their children through cell phones, and they will impose a firm curfew. This is often the only time that Omani teenagers might mingle with foreign teenagers, their common interests outside school bringing them together.

DAILY LIFE

In many ways daily life in Omani cities is very similar to that of the West, except for the early starts to complete morning prayers. Dawn prayers (*Fajr*) are the first prayers of the day, and begin before the sun rises. Mornings are spent preparing for the working day, perhaps including an early visit to the mosque, getting children off to school—they may be taken by car or catch the school bus near home—and traveling to work. Omanis break from their work during the day to attend to their prayers at noon (*Dhuhr*), and in the afternoon (*Asr*), whether privately in their workplace or at the local mosque. The late afternoon sees the start of the rush hour, with most businesses closing between 4:00 p.m. and 5:00 p.m. The fourth prayers of the day (*Maghrib*) take place at sunset, and the fifth (*Isha*) after dark.

While working men and women are out during the day, housewives will be attending to their

homes, cleaning or cooking, or supervising their domestic helpers while they carry out this work. The mother will go out to do her shopping at the *souq*, for fresh produce, and the local small grocery store or supermarket, while her children are in school. She may visit other female family members or friends at their houses, and will return home in time for the end of the school day.

Weekends and evenings are the only time available for socializing, visiting the wider family, and engaging in any other hobbies and activities. Families enjoy visiting local parks on the weekends, and picnics and barbecues are popular. It is not unusual to see people having picnics on the grass shoulders along the roadside, apparently oblivious to the traffic.

Shops stay open quite late in Oman. The shops of the *souq* close at about 9:00 p.m., and the

supermarkets and malls close at 10:00 p.m. During Ramadan and in preparation for Eid, shops will stay open as late as 1:00 a.m. Often the entire family will go out to buy groceries and other goods, if

they haven't been purchased during the day by the mother.

The main meal of the day is in the evening, and the whole family will gather to eat together and watch sitcoms on Omani TV afterward. The father and older sons go out for a short time to attend to their evening prayers at the mosque. Coffeehouses stay open until late into the night, and are regular meeting places for the menfolk in the evenings.

Rural life is quite different, with women staying at home and completing all the household chores while their husbands are out at work. Men rise early to go to the mosque and to get ready for a day of agricultural work, typically on date farms or, for those near the coast, fishing. Children will walk to the bus stop, or all the way to school, on their own. Most men come home at lunchtime for their meal and to pray; they will often sleep during the hottest part of the day before returning to work in the early afternoon. Children are generally left to their own devices once home from school, as the women are engaged in preparing for the return of the men in the early evening.

HEALTH CARE FOR OMANIS

In the past thirty-six years great progress has been made in the country's health care system, which now provides free or very low-cost medical care for all Omanis. The public hospitals are open to everyone, including expatriates; there are also military and private hospitals. The standards of medical care in Oman are now equal to those in the West, and there are no long waiting lists, but despite the new technology and the well-trained doctors many Omanis go abroad for major operations, particularly favoring the USA and the UK.

In recent years, obesity and other diseases associated with affluence and "bad habits" have become increasingly common in Oman, as in the neighboring countries. This is particularly the case in the urban areas of the country.

QAHWAH

Coffee, *qahwah*, is an important part of daily life in Oman. It is made from freshly roasted beans that have been crushed into a fine powder, with added spices. There is always a pot of thick, steaming coffee ready at mealtimes and when visitors arrive; in fact coffee used to be the only drink served before and after meals. It is served throughout the day, at home, in offices, and in hotels.

Omani coffee cups are very small, bowl-shaped, and often elaborately decorated. One tiny cup is usually all that is needed, as the coffee is very strong. It is always served black, often flavored with *hail* (cardamom), according to your host's personal taste, and will probably appear without any preamble or inquiry as to a visitor's own tastes. It is polite to accept the first cup, which is usually filled only halfway, never to the brim, and you won't be offered sugar. When you have had enough, and the coffeepot (*dallah*) comes around again, the polite way to refuse any more is to shake your empty cup gently from side to side. *Qahwah* is often served with something sweet, such as *halwa* or dates, and these sticky, sugary flavors work well with the bitterness of the hot coffee.

While *qahwah* is the traditional Omani drink, tea is also served at mealtimes and is available throughout the rest of the day in modern Oman. The preferred way of drinking it is black, in a small glass, with lots of sugar and occasionally with fresh sprigs of mint. One serving of this sweet, steaming hot brew is enough to refresh and revive even the most weary traveler.

chapter six

TIME OUT

Omanis love to spend time with their families and friends, whether the occasion is an impromptu picnic, a visit to the park, a walk through the bustling *souqs*, or just sitting outside a café and watching the world go by. The heat of the summer months drives those who can escape the city to do so, and others to cooler temperatures indoors, to enjoy eating and socializing at home.

As we have seen, coffee plays an important part in social life. Local coffeehouses provide entertainment for men and teenage boys throughout Oman.

Along with traditional beverages, these establishments provide *shisha* and an opportunity to play games such as backgammon with friends, inside or out.

Omani women and their young children generally socialize with their female friends and family in their homes. They also go clothes shopping together, and may go to restaurants or chain coffee shops in the shopping malls, but generally don't take part in the traditional coffeehouse culture.

CULTURAL ACTIVITIES
Museums

Oman has a rich heritage, and one of the government's policies is to maintain as much of Omani history as possible in order to allow the younger generations to learn about their past. There are many museums in the country, with some of the larger ones in Muscat, including the Muscat Gate Museum, which shows how the city has developed and changed both as a result of foreign invasion and through Oman's own strategies. The Museum of Omani Heritage has some particularly interesting displays on all the different aspects of life in Oman, as well as detailed archaeological information. It shows how the people from each area have lived through Oman's history, what their traditional trades were, and which are still practiced by them today.

Cinema

Trips to the cinema are very popular, and enjoyed by the whole family. Movies tend to be Western and Asian blockbusters, with subtitles in Arabic. Imported films are heavily censored, and whole sections of them may be cut out if they are considered not to meet Omani cultural or religious views. There are very few locally produced films. General screenings are not segregated, and men and women sit in the cinema together. Some cinemas have introduced a morning screening to cater to women, both Omani and expatriate.

Throughout a screening, patrons come and go, talk to each other, and take calls on their cell phones, chatting away oblivious to everyone around them. As soon as the credits appear the houselights come on and most people leave right away, as they have no interest in the credits.

Theater

While storytelling is a traditional pastime, passed down through the generations, Western-style drama doesn't have a long history in Oman. The first plays were put on in local schools in the 1970s, and were either in Arabic or, to a limited extent, in English; most were adapted from books and scripts from Egypt and Lebanon. The Muscat Youth troupe was formed in 1980, and consists of young Omanis trained by Arab actors.

In recent years there has been an attempt to bring more drama to Oman. The Al Fulaij Castle in Barka, once a military stronghold, has been converted into an open-air theater with state-of-the-art facilities by the Omani government, with the assistance of UNESCO. The seasonal performances staged there range from concerts by international orchestras to Arabic plays and folk dancing by local Omani groups.

Music

Music plays an important part in leisure time, with the playing of traditional musical instruments such as the *ud* (a five- or six-stringed instrument with a short neck) and the *tanbura* (a stringed instrument without a neck, plucked in the fashion of a harp), and the singing of traditional folk songs. At large events such as weddings and Eid celebrations, the men sing and dance in beautiful, rhythmic motions, just as their ancestors did. Dance is adapted as required by the event, with slow, solemn, swaying steps for religious occasions and fast, light-footed dancing for entertainment and enjoyment.

These musical traditions are so important to Omani culture that Sultan Qaboos has recently announced plans for the House of Musical Arts to be built in Qurm, which will feature a modern performance center to accommodate over a thousand people. The Oman Center for Traditional Music was created to encourage Omanis to keep these musical traditions alive through education, and includes a vast archive of photographic, audio, and video records of music, dancing, and singing throughout the country.

VISITING A MOSQUE

Special permission must be obtained before a non-Muslim is allowed into a mosque. There are very important guidelines to adhere to when visiting a mosque, even if you are only admiring the outside. Wear loose, modest clothing. Women should have their arms and shoulders covered and wear a skirt below the knee, or trousers. Men should wear trousers and a shirt, not shorts or short-sleeved T-shirts. If granted access to the interior of a mosque, women must cover their

hair with a scarf or shawl. Ensure that feet are clean, and leave your shoes in the appropriate place outside the door; you usually leave them on the steps, but there may be racks. There are separate entrances for men and women, who will usually be segregated inside the mosque. Once inside, never walk in front of a person who is praying, and if you are invited to sit down, kneel, with your feet tucked under you. It is offensive to show another person the soles of your feet. Remain quiet while you are inside, even if it is not prayer time, as many people attend the mosque for quiet contemplation and to read the Koran.

SHOPPING FOR PLEASURE

There is plenty of shopping to be done in Oman, whether in a traditional *souq* (market) or in one of the modern, Western-style malls. The malls cater to a wide range of tastes providing not only quite different goods from the traditional *souq*, but also places for socializing in the international coffee shops and restaurants. Most also have a cinema and other entertainment venues such as play centers for children.

Note that haggling is not done in the larger shops and shopping centers, and small signs stating that the shops operate a "fixed price" policy have started appearing in these in recent years.

The *souq* offers a vast array of products from traditional clothing, shoes, and jewelry to spices, incense, and other household items. Some, in the rural areas, have live animal auctions. Omanis enjoy the *souq* environment, and the men of the family often socialize at open-air cafés nearby

while the women attend to the actual marketing. The shops in the *souq* usually open in the morning around 9:00 a.m., and stay open until the early evening, usually closing for a few minutes at prayer time. On Fridays they may not open at all, or just in the late afternoon.

Bargaining

Haggling is very much part of the shopping experience in the *souq* and other small shops, and is expected; but take care to haggle only over items that are  worth it. Cheap items will have only a small margin for the seller, and it is a waste of time, for both parties, to try to get a lower price.

Shopkeepers are, of course, very experienced in the art of bargaining, but walking away is an excellent way of getting their attention, and thus a better price. They will tempt you to stay by offering cool drinks or tea. Don't go back unless you intend to buy, and then, once you have agreed on a price, go ahead and pay it—it's impolite not to do so. Make sure you have cash to pay with, as the majority of shops in the *souq* will not accept credit or debit cards.

SPORTS

Camels are a fundamental part of daily life for much of Oman and, as such, they are reared with care, especially those involved in racing. The racing season is from September to March or April, with the peak from late November through December. The Oman Camel Racing Federation organizes many races each season, mainly on public holidays and during the annual National Day celebrations. Horses also play an important role in recreation, with show jumping and dressage competitions held each winter at the Enam Equestrian show ground in Seeb, and at other venues throughout the country.

The vast extent of coastline and wonderful beaches make for an enthusiastic participation in water sports such as swimming, diving, and snorkeling, with even Omani women venturing into the sea for a dip. Oman was recently selected as the venue for the 2010 Asian Beach Games, which will bring together talented athletes from all over Asia and include windsurfing, swimming, beach volleyball, and dragon boat racing.

Football (soccer) is popular throughout the country, especially with younger men, and a win for the Omani team is cause for great celebration, with heavily decorated cars driving through the streets beeping their horns, flashing their lights, and proudly flying the Omani flag.

BEACHES

Oman's wonderfully long coastline is adorned with some of the most beautiful beaches in the Gulf. Most beaches are public and available to all to use. A small number of private beaches belong to hotels or are private or official property. One of the most popular areas for affluent Muscat Omanis to build their homes is near Qurm beach, a long stretch of uninterrupted sand.

People stare at women on the beach, although generally without any malice. This can be unnerving for a Western woman who wants to sunbathe or swim on a public beach—be sure to wear a one-piece swimsuit. Those Omani women who swim in the sea do so fully clothed, *abaya* and all. The large public beaches are more enjoyable for a stroll or a picnic than for sunbathing. The quieter, more out-of-the-way beaches are less likely to attract the local people, and are preferred by expatriates who live here. The alternative is to use a private beach associated with one of the hotels.

DINING OUT

Eating out remains one of the most popular social pastimes in Oman. You can find everything here, from the humblest coffee shop offering only hot and cold drinks to five-star restaurants serving haute cuisine. Oman is home to a large number

 of foreigners, and they have brought their eating habits with them. The result is a vast array of international cuisines available in the larger urban areas. In recent

years, fast-food chains, too, have been popping up all over the country.

Traditional Omani food consists of grilled or roasted meats—lamb, goat, or chicken—fish, rice, bread, and salads, usually followed by fresh fruit, desserts such as *Umm Ali* (the Arabic version of rice pudding), sweets, and coffee. Many of the dishes served in Oman are found throughout the Middle East, but Omani food contains more spice than the food of its neighbors. Grilled or fried fish and seafood are, not surprisingly, a local specialty, favorites being hammour, tuna, mackerel, and kingfish. Omanis will often order a whole large fish to share, with salads such as *tabbouleh* (bulgur wheat, finely chopped parsley, mint, and tomatoes) and *fattoush* (salad with crisp pieces of pita bread) as well as the Middle Eastern staple, *hummus* (a smooth dip made from chick peas, tahini, olive oil, and lemon juice). The favorite Omani sweet is *halwa*—a delicious, gelatinous, sugary sweet that is served either hot or cold, and is eaten with a spoon. It can be flavored with cardamom or dotted with pistachios.

Roadside cafés throughout Oman serve a popular Arabic staple—*shawarma,* a type of sandwich consisting of shredded meat, usually lamb or chicken, salad, and onions, wrapped in a

Lebanese pita bread. The meat is cooked on an upright revolving spit outside the restaurant. *Shawarma* are cheap, fast, filling, and delicious, with restaurants exercising their own flair by adding different ingredients, such as garlic sauce. When ordering their *shawarma*, patrons are often offered *falafel* (deep-fried balls of spiced, mashed chickpeas) as an addition. These can usually be supplied in a little bag right away, and are considered an Arabian version of fast food.

Most cafés and restaurants maintain high standards of hygiene and cleanliness, making it generally safe to eat and drink outside your hotel. However, it is advisable to take the usual precautions with prepared food. Make sure that meat and fish are cooked through and piping hot, and avoid anything that has been pre-prepared and left out at room temperature. Most water is bottled, although tap water is safe to drink—but don't take ice in it, or in any other cold drink.

Etiquette

Men wearing *dishdasha* will roll their sleeves up to their elbows before beginning their meal, and eat using their right hand only. Forearms are rested on the table between mouthfuls. Mealtimes are for eating, so there is little conversation once the food has reached the table. If you want to use a knife and fork in a café or small restaurant, you can ask for them, but they may not even have any.

It is polite to finish eating at the same time as your companions. Diners will get up to wash their hands as soon as they have finished. Restaurants will have one or more hand basins at the rear for washing, but no towel or dryer. Tissues from the table can be used to dry your hands.

NIGHTLIFE

Bars and nightclubs are very limited in Oman, as alcohol is only served in the hotels in the main cities, catering mainly to expatriates and tourists. Muslims are not permitted to drink alcohol, although Omanis are allowed into bars. While visitors are permitted to drink alcohol, there is a zero-tolerance drunk-driving policy in Oman, and the penalties, if you are caught, are severe. Public drunken behavior is unacceptable, and again the consequences are serious, including arrest and deportation.

chapter seven

TRAVEL, HEALTH, & SAFETY

Oman enjoys an unusual position in the world in that it is generally crime free and a safe place to visit. Of course there is some crime, but the strong Omani police force deals with problems quickly and efficiently. Foreigners can feel at ease as long as they understand the laws and abide by them. Compared to some of its neighboring Gulf countries, Oman is also a safer place to drive.

ROADS AND TRAFFIC

The extensive modern Omani road system, which covers all the lowland areas, is only forty years old, and the road from Muscat to Salalah was only finished in 1984. Only the mountainous areas have roads that are not tarred, and although it is possible for ordinary sedans to drive on the mountain roads, the average life span of these cars will not be long.

In Muscat the traffic, especially during the morning rush hour between 7:00 and 9:00 a.m., can be very dense. In the countryside, the traffic

RENTING A CAR

Making arrangements to rent a car is a relatively simple task. Many of the major car rental agencies have branches in Oman, and there are also local companies.

- You will need your driver's license (licenses from most countries are accepted) and your credit card.
- Make certain that the insurance agreement you sign is comprehensive and covers personal accident as well.
- Car seats for children may be available, but it is better to bring your own.
- A larger agency will have both a better selection of cars and a more accessible roadside assistance service.
- Speed limits are clearly marked, but watch out for the sudden changes from 70 mph (120 kmh) on the highways to 50 mph (80 kmh) in built-up areas.

is light throughout the day. Thursday afternoons are also very busy, as everyone finishes work for the weekend and hurries home. Generally, visitors will find driving in Oman a pleasant experience; but should be wary if it rains, even if the rain appears distant. Owing to the rocky nature of the ground, there is a danger of flash flooding, which should be taken very seriously. If you are driving a large, four-wheel-drive vehicle, you should be very cautious before attempting to cross any flooded area, especially where the water is flowing fast. If in doubt, wait and ask someone familiar with the locality if it is safe before crossing.

Following the devastation of Cyclone Gonu, which ravaged Oman in 2007, many of the modern roads and bridges needed to be rebuilt.

Driving

It is likely that your first experience of Omani driving will be on the journey from the airport to downtown Muttrah or Muscat. After the hustle of the airport it is an almost surreal experience to glide down a gently undulating, modern, six-lane highway, with immaculately landscaped gardens on both sides (but not a gardener in sight), at precisely the 70 mph (120 kmh) speed limit. Above this limit an insistent beep will be emitted from the dashboard. All cars in Oman are fitted with this warning device, and it is against the law to tamper with it. It is also technically against the law to drive in Oman in a dirty car, and you could potentially be fined for doing so.

The use of indicators is selective, and many drivers do not use them as a way of signaling their intent, turning without warning. Drivers who flash their lights are telling you to get out of their way. Traffic lights are respected, although drivers behind you will honk their horn the moment the light turns green. Try to ignore them.

Speed limits are generally obeyed, as fines are handed out by the police who regularly patrol the roads. Both fixed and movable speed cameras are in place throughout the country to catch speeding drivers. Seat belts must be worn at

all times, and talking on a cell phone while driving is also against the law.

Omanis are not used to driving in any conditions other than clear ones. Morning fog can cause mayhem on the roads, as will any sort of rain, including the lightest shower, and sandstorms. Be extremely cautious while driving in these conditions. Drivers put on their hazard warning lights while they are moving, supposedly to show where they are; Westerners often think these lights are on a stationary vehicle.

While driving in the urban areas of Oman, visitors will notice that everything is immaculately clean, with no trash in sight. In Muttrah and older parts of Muscat especially, the roads are lined at intervals with huge, beautiful pots of flowers; in inland towns there are statues and pots by the roadside, and even in remote villages in the countryside there are patches of greenery.

If you rent a four-wheel drive and go for a drive in the mountains, be aware that you will be

expected to give a free lift to absolutely anybody who is waiting by the side of the mountain tracks, along with their chickens, eggs, and sacks of dates. Also note that your vehicle will probably have a short length of clear plastic tubing in the glove box. An unwritten rule is that if you come across someone who has run out of fuel, you should stop and offer them some gas from your tank. It's out with the tube to siphon some of your fuel into the other car, and the other party will know exactly how to accomplish this!

Parking

Generous parking lots are normally provided around government ministries, embassies, major supermarkets, airports, banks, and shopping areas. You have to pay for parking in some of these places by means of orange coin-operated ticket machines; the ticket should be displayed on the driver's side of your dashboard. Check the dashboards of other cars parked in the area if you are not sure if you have to pay. Shopping malls have free parking garages, often in the basement, with the added benefit of shade. It is not always clear where these car parks are, and it may require a couple of trips round the block to find the entrance.

In older developments the parking areas may be less generous, and in some areas around office blocks you may find that every space is filled. Double parking is illegal, though many people do so for a few minutes while popping into  the bank, for example. Reversing down any road is also illegal, but it does happen occasionally. Always be aware of what's around you, and keep your eyes open for the unexpected.

Accidents

If you are involved in an accident, both parties must stop and wait for the police to arrive. In the cities and main towns, there are a lot of police patrols, and you will probably have two policemen with you within ten minutes—often far sooner. It is probably safest to wait inside your car, in the cool, with your hazard warning lights flashing, until the police arrive. If any parties require medical assistance, the police will call an ambulance.

The police will need details of your driver's license and insurance. Keeping the registration of one's car valid requires an annual fee, and the car must be insured to complete the paperwork. Hence almost everyone with a car in Oman has insurance, including visitors from neighboring countries who have brought their own car with them. Almost all policemen speak English, and you will find them courteous and polite, but firm if you have done anything wrong. There is zero tolerance toward driving while under the influence of alcohol or drugs, and such an offense is treated with the utmost severity. Once both parties have given their version of events, it may take the police some time to complete the paperwork required for their records. You are usually told to wait in your car unless it is unsafe to drive, in which case the police will arrange a tow truck to remove it. After an accident, you may be required to go to the nearest police station to make a further statement. All police stations in Oman are well maintained, clean, and air-conditioned. It is illegal to offer a bribe to a policeman.

Pedestrians

Except in the cool winter months, there are very few pedestrians about. People don't generally walk very far, and the majority of drivers park as close as possible to their destination. The pedestrian will find that drivers tend to obey the speed limit and the stoplights; blowing through a red light will result in a severe penalty. There are Western-style zebra crossings at regular intervals in the cities and main towns. It is in your interest to use them, but do so with caution. Drivers will usually stop to allow a woman to cross the road at any point, especially if she is covered or has children with her.

TRANSPORTATION

Buses, Coaches, and Minibuses

Bus and coach transportation is organized nationally by the Oman National Transportation Corporation (ONTC), which has a large maintenance base on the old international airport at Azaiba, about three miles east of Seeb

International Airport. The ONTC now has a vast number of modern buses and coaches, with routes all over Oman. The main bus terminal is at Ruwi, in the center of the Ruwi Valley, which stretches inland from Muttrah into the mountains and contains the majority of businesses and banks. From here buses depart at regular times during the day and night, to local destinations, to connect with every major town in Oman, and also to further afield, south to Salalah, approximately 620 miles (1000 km) away, and north to Dubai, about 370 miles (600 km). The long-distance coaches to Dubai and Salalah have air-conditioning and a toilet, and also make stops at desert guesthouses. Ticket prices are modest. Fares are paid to the driver; try to have the correct amount.

There is an unofficial airport bus that leaves hourly throughout the day, except at lunchtime, from near the fish market on Muttrah Corniche and goes to Seeb *souq* via Seeb International Airport.

Private Taxis

Taxis are painted a distinctive white and orange, and are plentiful throughout Oman. You hail one from the side of the road, or pick one up outside a shopping center or hotel. Almost all are in good to excellent condition, although not all have functioning seat belts. They are all driven and owned by Omanis, and their fares, compared with other countries around the Gulf, are quite high. There are no meters, so a price must be discussed and agreed upon before you even get into the taxi. Visitors should note that hotels don't have courtesy cars, so it's usually necessary to take a taxi to your hotel.

There are several private taxi companies with fleets of cars that serve the cities. These can be booked in advance, but the bookings cannot always be relied upon, so it is better to call a short while before you require your taxi. These taxis are metered, so prices don't need to be agreed on in advance.

There's a cheaper alternative, known as Jebel taxis. These are simple pickup trucks that bring people down from the mountains, and are extremely basic. They are often also used for transporting animals to market before picking up paying passengers. To get a ride, just flag one down, climb in the back, and pay when you get off. Few Westerners use the Jebel taxi service, the exceptions being mainly the impecunious young, who become adept at spotting them at all times of the day or night. Watch out for goat droppings!

Aircraft

Oman Air operates a variety of twin-engine turboprop aircraft known as ATRs to provide a service to such locations as Khasab in the Musandam,

Sohar, Sur, and Masirah. Oman Air uses Boeing
737 twin jets to conduct a shuttle three times a day
to Salalah. There are frequent flights to all
destinations around the Gulf. Oman Air flies to
Pakistan, India, and Sri Lanka.

Most of the major airlines use Seeb International
Airport. Tickets should be purchased in advance
either from one of Oman Air's offices in the cities or
at the desk at the airport. Always carry your passport
on any flight, internal or international. While travel
within Oman does not require anything more than
a tourist visa, you should check visa regulations if
flying out of Oman into a neighboring country.

Ships

Cruise ships call quite often and dock in the harbor
of Muttrah and in the port at Salalah. These tend to
be used by foreign visitors rather than Omanis.
There is a new high-speed ferry service that
operates between Muscat and Khasab. Trips are

scheduled three
times a week at
10:00 a.m., with
returns on three
alternate days. An
additional ferry is
to be put into
operation shortly.

WHERE TO STAY

Hotels

All the major hotel chains are represented in Oman, primarily in Muscat, and with some in Salalah. There is something for just about every budget in Muscat. Rates are usually nonnegotiable at check-in, but there may be some flexibility in the price when booking in advance. Summer is low season, so rates are more reasonable then. Passports are required when checking in at all Omani hotels.

There are smaller and more modest hotels in Sur, Sohar, Nizwa, and Buraimi, and desert hotels or guesthouses on the route to Salalah. All have pools except the smaller desert hotels.

Apartments

For those planning a longer stay, it is fairly easy to find an apartment in Muscat, and even a villa. Details are available in the local newspapers. It is always worth doing a visual check of any apartment or villa, both inside and out. Also look around for schools and mosques—both can get busy and very noisy at certain times of the day, and nearby roads may get clogged during prayer time and at the start and end of the school day.

Rents are detailed in your tenancy contract, and do not usually include utilities. Apartments are rented either furnished or unfurnished. A furnished apartment is more usually in a block of "hotel apartments." These are available on long or short leases, and often have the same in-house facilities as a hotel, such as a maid service and laundry facilities, included in the price. Don't forget to check on the parking situation; many apartments have allocated parking spaces for residents.

HEALTH

Generally, Oman is a healthy place, and you are more likely to suffer from sunburn that anything else. The tap water throughout the country comes from desalination plants, and is safe to drink in the cities, but somewhat tasteless. Be wary of tap water in more rural areas, which should be boiled before drinking; many visitors like a bottled water called Tanuf, which comes from a well at the base of Jebel Akhdar near Nizwa, and is very pleasant to drink.

The standard of hospitals, their equipment, and the doctors and nursing staff is very high, and getting even better. There are also many private clinics located where expatriates live. Oman has a good distribution of rural health facilities as well: don't be surprised if you drive up some track, seemingly in the middle of nowhere, and come across a small but modern-looking clinic!

It is recommended that expatriates and visitors take antimalarial tablets. It is essential to start the course before you actually arrive in Oman. Although mosquitoes are not a big problem, there have been fatalities due to malaria in the past twenty years.

Swimming in the sea is generally safe, and the water is normally quite clear. There have been instances of swimmers being stung by the highly dangerous Portuguese man-of-war jellyfish, but this is a very rare occurrence. Look out for beached jellyfish, as these are still dangerous. There are other animals in Oman that are dangerous but usually not deadly to man. Scorpions, snakes, and camel spiders are relatively common throughout the country. Always give shoes that have been outside a good shake to make sure that no creepy crawlies have crept in.

Swimming in the mountain *wadis* is also generally safe, and is sometimes the only way to make progress while walking in these areas. While most *wadis* are dry drainage channels, some contain water throughout the year as they are fed by subterranean aquifers. However, it is not sensible to swim in still or stagnant water. When in the *wadis*, keep a weather eye open for towering clouds or distant rain showers. If a flash flood comes down the *wadi* you will not be able to outrun it.

Home Remedies

Generally Omanis like to use traditional home remedies for common ailments rather than buying branded medicine. They will mix honey and the juice of local limes to make a cough syrup, drink the water used to boil rice to settle an upset stomach and help to stop diarrhea, and eat spicy food to break a fever.

SAFETY

Oman is a very well-respected country worldwide. It is generally safe and free of terrorism, both homegrown and imported. It is responsible, along with Iran, for the safe passage of tankers and other shipping through the Strait of Hormuz. As previously mentioned, Oman has a sizeable police force and also a well equipped army, air force and navy. The Oman Intelligence Service was developed along British lines and is quite sophisticated.

The Royal Oman Police force is about twenty thousand strong, and very well trained; all policemen go to the Nizwa Police Academy and there is an excellent distribution of police stations throughout the country. The police force includes the fire service; it has a fleet of very modern patrol boats, and fleet of modern aircraft and helicopters, which also serve as SAR (search and rescue) helicopters. Visitors will see many policemen, usually patrolling in their cars and generally concentrating on traffic offenses.

Most Omani men wear the traditional *khunjar*, a large dagger worn around the waist as a sign of manhood, although this should not be understood as a threat or a challenge. In the mountains, many men still carry a rifle, and if the visitor has the good fortune to attend a wedding in the mountains, there will probably be some celebratory gunfire.

By Western standards, crime is virtually nonexistent. However, as always, it is wise to take sensible precautions wherever you are.

Women

Women of any nationality are highly respected in Omani society, as long as they are modestly dressed, and there is very little harassment of women. Any woman entering a bank, post office, or shop may—and will be expected to—go straight to the front of the line and be served without waiting.

However, a female visitor wearing skimpy or revealing clothes in public will be considered most improper and immodest. The police may tell her to leave the public area, and she may well be fined. There have even been occasions where women have been deported for improper dress.

chapter eight

BUSINESS BRIEFING

Doing business in Oman is, in general, relatively easy, although it does have its own unique challenges. The pace of business dealings generally can be much slower than in the West, and there are often delays with official paperwork due to the amount of bureaucracy in the public sector. It is essential to stay up-to-date with laws and procedures, and this can be done via the individual Web sites of the various government departments, which are available in both Arabic and English.

A major part of Oman's long-term commercial strategy concerns the industrial sector of the economy, and in 1995 the "Oman 2020" initiative was launched, detailing the plans for progress. These include the setting up of new industrial concerns that will make Oman a player in the global economy, along with the acquisition of skills necessary for Omanis to work throughout these industries. The government's far-reaching policy includes provisions to increase the amount of foreign investment as well as encouraging private enterprise.

There are modern meeting rooms and business centers in the larger hotels throughout the country with satellite television, fax and printing services, and Internet connections. Large businesses are equipped with all the trappings of modern technology.

Government offices are open five days a week, Saturday to Wednesday, from 7:30 a.m. to 2:30 p.m. Private offices are open from 9:00 a.m. to 5:00 p.m., and work either a five-day week, in line with the government departments and schools, or six days, with Friday being the only day off. Some private

companies still work on the "split shift" system, opening early and closing at 1:00 p.m., so that workers can go home for lunch and to rest, then reopening at 4:00 p.m. and working until 7:00 p.m. Working hours are reduced during the month of Ramadan, when most businesses open about an hour later and many close earlier in the afternoon. Government departments also close earlier during

Ramadan. During public holidays such as Eid and National Day, all businesses close for the entirety of the holiday.

BUSINESS CULTURE

There are many large, well-established family businesses in Oman, which continue to grow and monopolize certain sectors of the local market. However, increasing numbers of multinational companies are setting up as new legislation is passed to make this easier. There are also many medium-sized and small businesses, with plenty of these being sole proprietorships.

Foreign companies based in Oman must have a local agent or partner who holds a majority stake in the company. Agents usually have several different companies under their sponsorship, as they do not play any part in the day-to-day running of the business and are paid an annual fee for their services. A partner will generally be involved in only one or two companies, as he will play a more active role and may have invested his own funds in the company.

When problems arise, it is important to have a friendly, open-minded approach rather than become frustrated with the process. Issuing ultimatums generally doesn't solve the problem or speed things up and, in fact, may cause a business deal to be canceled altogether.

While many people speak English in Oman, communication problems can occur in some of the government offices, as most workers will speak Arabic with only a limited amount of English. Most companies have a public relations officer (PRO) who is responsible for dealings with the government at a low level. His jobs include organizing visas, following up on documentation that is pending, and creating a network within the relevant departments that will help future dealings move more quickly.

Oman has a zero-tolerance policy toward corruption.

THE IMPORTANCE OF PERSONAL RELATIONS

Personal relationships play a major role in every sphere in Oman, and active networking and maintaining contacts are imperative in order to progress in the business arena. Meeting people is essential to create these contacts, and happens both during working hours and after the day is done. Introductions and personal contacts can help to open useful doors. Businesspeople carry a plentiful supply of business cards, handing them out to everyone they meet and expecting to get one back in exchange to add to their database.

Business in Oman is often done on trust, so knowing the right person in the right position is important for success. Once a useful business connection has been established, it is vital that good relations are maintained if the parties want to work together in the future. Good relations help with everything, from creating new business, to getting important paperwork completed and receiving payments in a timely fashion. As we have seen, it is common for things to take time in Oman, and having these key contacts can help speed up the process. Just talking to the right person can move things along.

Because Oman is a hierarchical society, personal connections and family ties can play an important role. Views of what may constitute nepotism are different in Oman from what is acceptable in the West.

LOCAL AND FOREIGN LABOR

The workforce in Oman is made up of more than just the local Omanis. With its proximity to the subcontinent, Oman utilizes both skilled and unskilled labor from India, Sri Lanka, and Pakistan. Oman also has close ties with the rest of the GCC countries and nationals from these countries can work, own certain businesses in certain sectors, purchase land, and live in Oman without the need for a residence visa.

Unions are not permitted in Oman. The Ministry of Manpower is responsible for all workers in the country, whether foreign or Omani, and the Labor Law determines all aspects of employees' rights. Working hours are carefully monitored, although overtime is permitted in certain circumstances. The Omanization program aims to encourage more local businesses to employ Omanis in roles previously filled by foreign workers, and a visa is now granted to a foreign worker only when there is no Omani to take the job. There are several schemes in place to increase the skill sets, such as computer literacy, of preuniversity and postgraduate Omanis.

OFFICE ETIQUETTE
Despite the heat, formal dress is essential when doing business in Oman. A jacket and tie are required for men, with a long-sleeved shirt. Most men will remove their jacket once outside the building, so the long sleeves are important. Men with long

hair, piercings (including earrings), and visible tattoos may be considered unprofessional. Women should wear a suit either with trousers—the safer option—or with a skirt that is well below the knee. Suits can be fitted, but never tight or revealing. Wear a long-sleeved blouse or top, and avoid plunging necklines and see-through fabrics.

Initial communications must be of a formal nature, whether speaking over the telephone, via e-mail, or meeting in person. Correct titles should be used at all times, as failure to do so will be considered rude and will affect the remainder of the business relationship. Ministers should be addressed as "Your Excellency." It is acceptable to use the English "Mr." if the correct title is not known, but it is better to do your research first and observe the correct formalities.

Business gifts are generally given on certain occasions. For example, it is polite to offer some form of edible gift to mark the Eid holidays—dates are a popular choice, as are sweets and nuts. It is important to offer a gift that is not very expensive, as the recipient will be inclined to return a gift of the same value. Omanis like to receive gifts from your home country, such as a local craft object or some delicacy that is appreciated where you come from, as long as it conforms with Omani cultural guidelines. If you receive a gift from an Omani business colleague, it is polite to give something in return. If you are not able to do so at that moment, send a small token once you have returned home.

WOMEN IN BUSINESS

An increasing number of women are in important business positions in Omani society, while plenty are in the more traditional office jobs. However, the role of women has not changed completely, and they are still expected to fulfill their duties as wives and mothers. The priority is the home, so working and advancing in her chosen career can be a challenge for an Omani woman.

For a man, it is important to observe the usual cultural restrictions when meeting and dealing with women in the business place. Avoid any touching, including shaking hands, unless the woman offers her hand first. Maintain appropriate personal space, and avoid any form of intimate contact. It is not appropriate to invite a female business colleague out for dinner or for coffee outside the workplace—although she may invite you, along with other colleagues or other business contacts. This is unusual, however, and entertaining visiting businesspeople will often be delegated by a woman to male colleagues.

MEETINGS

First contacts with potential business partners are usually made in writing and, with increasing frequency, by e-mail. Cold calls are not generally accepted, and a written form of introduction about your company and your goods or services is preferable. It is important to do your research and address your correspondence to a named appropriate individual. A general letter to "Dear Sir" will not reach the correct person, and there will be no reply from the company. It is important to follow up your initial correspondence to ensure that it has reached your contact; a phone call is appropriate here.

Appointments should be made well in advance of actual meeting dates, and it is imperative to call ahead to confirm the day and time. Initial meetings will be formal, and usually held in your contact's place of business. First impressions are very important to Omanis, and you will be judged on this first meeting, so it is essential to wear proper business attire and to conduct yourself in a professional manner. Address your contacts by title, unless they say otherwise. Business cards will be produced on introduction.

As with everything in Omani life, the personal relationship is considered above all else, and it is important to observe the social niceties before getting down to business. Your host will first want to ensure that you are comfortable, will offer coffee and other light refreshment, and will expect to have some small talk. Stick to safe topics, such as your visit to Oman, your good first impressions, where you are staying, and how your journey was. Avoid subjects that might cause your host to be uncomfortable, such as religion, politics, and any negativity about Oman or its people. It is inadvisable to mention your host's family, unless he brings up the subject first, and you should never ask after his wife or other females in his family. As the relationship develops, and if you are introduced to your host's family, this may become acceptable

Meetings in Oman can often be lengthy, with breaks for more refreshments or for your host to attend to his prayers. People can come and go, especially if you're meeting in your contact's office, and telephone calls may be taken, especially on cell phones. The conversation may be interrupted many times, and this can be quite distracting. Don't look at your watch, as this will be taken as a sign of boredom and considered rude. Simply pick up your conversation at the point at which you were disturbed. Schedule appointments with plenty of time in between, as most will turn out to be longer than expected.

Follow up your first meeting with a telephone call or by e-mail. Keep in touch, and send a reminder of what has been discussed or agreed upon during your meeting. This helps to avoid possible misunderstandings later, and will also firm up the personal relationship. Once the first meetings have been held in a formal business setting and you know your contact a little better, you may meet outside the business place, but it is best to leave such an arrangement to him.

At the end of a meeting, it is appropriate to shake hands with those present (again, if there are women, follow their lead and do not shake hands unless they offer to do so). There may be a few more minutes of small talk, and your contact may walk you to the door or elevator. Say that you will be in touch, and how you plan to do so. If your contact's cell phone number is given on his business card, then it's fine to call him on that number during business hours.

PRESENTATIONS

With the introduction of user-friendly modern technology, a flexible style of presentation is becoming more common than a formal event. During a small, informal presentation Omanis like to talk and engage with their visitors in a friendly, relaxed manner, and the session is likely to be interrupted by questions and phone calls.

A formal presentation, such as to a large number of businesspeople or government officials, will be a more serious and regulated affair, with a secretary present to take notes. There may still be some disruptions, but these will be less likely in a meeting-room setting, and people will have set aside this time to attend. However, if you do find yourself being interrupted and the flow broken, it is essential to be accommodating and, above all, to be patient. It may feel as though you're being ignored, but that won't be the case.

The seniority of the people who attend your presentation will depend on various factors, including the size of the business you are dealing with, the amount of business that you will bring to the company, and the amount of investment involved. It will usually be middle management or department heads or their deputies who attend this sort of meeting. If the CEO of the company is present, the atmosphere will be different. There will be less socializing, and time may be tight. Ask beforehand how much time you will have for your presentation, remembering to factor in some minutes for any social interaction at the beginning and end as well as for interruptions. Allow another few minutes at the end for questions.

Wait for introductions to be made and everyone to settle, then begin the presentation right away. Keep it as short as possible and insure that copies of any notes, tables of figures, or statistics associated with the presentation are available for attendees. If the senior person leaves the room or receives a phone call, stop, and resume when he returns or hangs up.

Don't try to win over your audience with jokes. Omani humor is quite different from Western humor, and meanings can be lost in translation, making for an awkward situation. Omani jokes can appear extremely racist or sexist to Westerners. They don't translate well into English, and often sound far worse than they really are. The same is true for English jokes translated into Arabic. It's also best to avoid personal stories, unless they directly relate to the subject matter being presented.

NEGOTIATIONS

Negotiations can be a difficult area, and it is important to take several factors into account from the beginning. The first of these is the different understanding of aspects such as deadlines. A deadline can be considered set in stone in the West, but Omanis will see it more as a guideline or approximate date. The second factor is that in Oman everything is considered to be negotiable—haggling occurs in all the different spheres of life, and is expected in business as well. You will be expected to start high and then come back later with either a lower price or lower expectations. Never enter negotiations with fixed ideas. You must be flexible, and willing to alter aspects of your proposal.

Negotiations often take several attempts to find the right balance. It is important to stay in regular contact and to keep discussing as many options as you can find until you reach agreement. It is perfectly acceptable to go away from initial discussions to reflect and then to come back with a new offer later on.

You will usually be negotiating with middle management unless you are dealing with a small company or it is a particularly large contract that is under discussion. Middle managers will then liaise with senior management and come back

with further changes. Of all the aspects of doing business in Oman, finding a compromise during negotiations can be one of the most time-consuming. It is important to be patient and flexible at this stage.

CONTRACTS

Contracts should be as comprehensive as possible, with all the fine details clearly set out. A contract with a foreign company will probably be drafted in English, with an Arabic version prepared later. In the event of court proceedings, English contracts, as well as other paperwork in English, will need to be translated and notarized before being presented in court.

Contracts are binding in Oman, as in the West. In fact, a simple handshake on agreement is considered to bind the two parties, but is harder to enforce and much more complicated to take to court. It is best to have everything in writing, and details that are agreed to verbally should be followed up with written correspondence to ensure that all parties understand what is expected of them. Court proceedings are lengthy and expensive so it is essential to include a clause agreeing on the use of an arbitrator to be appointed in case of any dispute.

It can take time to get contracts signed and it is important to continue following up until you receive the signed contract. It is advisable to wait until you have a signed contract before starting the service or providing the goods detailed in your agreement.

DEALING WITH GOVERNMENT

The Omani government controls public services. It is responsible for the appointment of heads of public-sector corporations. It is also responsible for the Omanization program that is in place throughout Oman, which ensures that a certain number of Omanis are employed in all sectors of the Omani economy. There are laws in place that prevent government ministers from holding positions in private-sector companies that do business with the Omani government.

When dealing with the government, you will usually be meeting with middle management. Expect some delays as your proposal or contract moves through to more senior government officials. It is illegal to offer a bribe to any government employee or official, and the penalties for doing so are severe.

chapter nine

COMMUNICATING

LANGUAGE

Arabic is Oman's official language, and is spoken throughout the country. There are two forms of Arabic here: classical Arabic (or, more recently, Modern Standard Arabic), and the local Omani dialect. The classical form is the language of the Koran, and is also used in books, the media, and official documents. Modern Standard Arabic is studied in local schools, with English taught as a second language. People in the Gulf countries speak similar dialects of Arabic, and have no difficulty understanding each other. Out of the Gulf region, however, accents are different, and the words used are not always the same. If they are in another Arabic-speaking country, most Arabic speakers are able to switch from their own native dialect to classical Arabic.

Colloquial Arabic is used in daily life, whether in the shops, at home, in a business setting, or in government offices. However, most written correspondence, official documentation, and forms are in classical Arabic. It is important for Omanis to be fluent in both, and they switch seamlessly from one to the other.

In a business setting, English will generally be spoken with the same ease as Arabic. The Omani upper and middle classes speak it well. Conversations are often in a combination of Arabic and English, adapted to suit the audience. In Oman's cities English is widely, if not fluently, spoken, and it is possible to get by as a tourist without speaking any Arabic at all. Omanis will appreciate any effort on the part of the visitor to communicate in Arabic, however, even if it is just a basic greeting or a simple "*Shukran*" ("Thank you"). It is perfectly acceptable to greet an Omani in Arabic and then continue the rest of your conversation in English, and the gesture will be appreciated. In more rural areas of the country, a few words of Arabic are recommended for basic communication. The English spoken in these places will be very basic, perhaps nonexistent. Any attempt on your part at speaking Arabic will be greeted warmly, and by a patient audience.

Language schools in Oman offer courses to foreigners in Modern Standard Arabic as well as teaching the colloquial form, which is particularly important for spoken Arabic. The other option is to take lessons from a private tutor. You will find schools listed in the English daily papers and local magazines, and tutors in the classified sections.

CONVERSATION AND RESPECT

Omanis place huge importance on people and relationships. It is therefore important to address people with respect and courtesy, regardless of their social standing or how well you know them. On walking into a room, an Omani will greet everyone there rather than just the person they've come to see. Everyone in that room will respond. It is of great importance in Oman to offer the correct amount of respect to people in senior positions, whether in a family or a business setting. Older family members are always offered a personal greeting first. It is essential that foreigners understand and appreciate these social norms if they want to integrate themselves into Omani culture.

Once the greetings are complete, Omanis will often ask about each other's health and that of their children. Men do not discuss each other's wives or unmarried female family members. It is important to be courteous without being overfamiliar. There are always a few minutes of small talk at the beginning of conversation, whether it's a social call or a business one.

Omanis appreciate a respective audience, and usually have a lot to say. Social conversations tend to be long and enjoyable for all concerned. Certain topics, such as politics, are generally avoided in social situations for fear of causing offense or, even worse, starting an argument. In Omani culture there is no such thing as saying "Hello" in passing—it would be considered discourteous not to stop and exchange pleasantries, regardless of how busy you may be or what else is going on. It is also important to introduce anyone who may be with you, with a brief explanation of who they are.

BODY LANGUAGE

It is important to display the correct body language while talking with Omanis. Conversation usually involves hand gestures and can be very animated while highlighting an important point in a story. Slumping or slouching in a chair is considered rude, and seems to show a lack of interest in the person and the conversation; sitting up straight and leaning slightly toward the speaker is the preferred position, and shows interest and respect.

In a group setting, you should take care that you don't have your back to anyone, as that person might assume you were ignoring them and could take offense. If it is absolutely unavoidable, apologize to that person in advance. Never put your feet up on a chair or desk, and if you cross your legs you should ensure that the soles of your feet are not visible.

Omanis often sit on the floor, whether in a *majlis* or while eating. In these settings, you must remove your shoes at the door. When men sit down, they tuck their feet underneath themselves so that they are resting on their heels. Women sit with their feet to one side. Omanis are completely at ease in these positions, though Westerners can find them uncomfortable after a time. You should never sit on the floor cross-legged, or with your legs straight out in front of you.

THE MEDIA

Omanis get their daily news and information from several sources, the most popular ones being the Arabic newspapers and the local television station. There are several daily newspapers in both Arabic and English, as well as a large number of locally published magazines, all of which are widely available in shops, supermarkets, bookshops, and gas stations.

All printed publications are subject to approval by the Federal Ministry of Information, including all books and magazines that are  imported from abroad. The government has the right to censor local publications so that they conform to Omani cultural standards. Culturally sensitive "blacking out" is often seen in imported publications, with scantily clad women and other offensive pictures literally blacked out with a marker pen. It is common for entire pages containing offensive material to be torn out of imported magazines.

The main daily Arabic newspapers are *Al Watan* and *Al Shabiba*. English newspapers such as the *Oman Daily Observer, Oman Tribune,* and *Times of Oman* are widely read throughout the country and act as one of the main sources of information for English-speaking residents. Most of the daily newspapers have a special edition on a Friday with additional social and cultural information. *The Week* is a popular independent weekly English newspaper that covers news, business, sports, and lifestyle events in Oman.

There is only one locally broadcast television station, with the majority of television viewed in Oman coming via satellite. Broadcast in Arabic, Oman TV is the government-run local television station, and it reaches every corner of the land. Features include religious programs, drama, documentaries, and quiz shows, along with local news and announcements about public holidays, prayer times during Ramadan, and the call to prayer. Local restaurants and coffee shops often have a television tuned to Oman TV for their patrons. Most people watch some form of satellite television in their homes. There is no censorship of satellite channels, and they are available to any resident who can pay the subscription fee. Satellite packages include the major international news channels. Satellite channels are also available in hotels throughout the country.

The main radio broadcasters are owned by the government, with one privately owned station currently on air. The state-owned stations are *Radio Sultanate of Oman* (Arabic), *Al Shabab Radio* (Arabic), and *Radio Oman—English FM*. Oman's first independent radio station, *Hala FM*, launched in 2007, provides listeners with Arabic music and entertainment.

SERVICES
Telephone
Oman has a modern telephone system, which makes calling abroad simple and efficient. There

are rarely any difficulties connecting to the rest of the world. Directory inquiries can be made in Arabic or English by calling 198.

Cell phone networks work throughout most of Oman and work on GSM. There are some more remote areas where service is not available. Prepaid cards are available at shops, supermarkets, and gas stations, and there will usually be a sign in the window or on the door where they are sold. It is possible to have a postpaid or billed line, requiring a visit to Oman Mobile and completing some paperwork. You will need to have a residence visa to apply for one of these lines. The prepaid lines are more common, and a SIM card can be purchased by visitors.

Pay phones are available throughout the country. Most shops and restaurants will allow you to use their phone in an emergency and for a short call, often without charge. However, it is appropriate to offer to pay for the call. OmanTel offers a very useful prepaid calling card called Jibreen, which works on landlines and pay phones, with prices starting at OR 1.5.

EMERGENCY

Royal Oman Police   All Emergency Services   999

Mail

The postal system in Oman is fairly reliable for both local and international mail. Local letters take one or two days. International airmail takes about five to seven days to Europe and ten to fourteen days to North America. Most outgoing mail reaches its destination without any complications. Important packages and papers are usually sent by courier, either a local company or one of the more recognized international ones, to ensure safe delivery, although the post office also offers a registered service requiring a signature on delivery.

Incoming mail is subject to stringent checks at customs, and packages are often opened to check their contents. Books, CDs, and DVDs are reviewed to ensure that they conform to Omani laws and do not contain any illegal material. Offending items will be confiscated by customs. There may be a customs duty to pay on receipt of a package, depending on the value determined by the customs officer.

There is no mail delivery to homes or businesses; all mail goes into post office boxes at the post office. In order to receive mail, it should have your post office box number, the city, zip code, and country.

Internet

Oman has a modern Internet system, and access to the Web is available throughout the cities and urban areas. There are Internet cafés as well as Wi-Fi hot spots in certain malls and coffee shops where anyone with a wireless-enabled laptop can get online. All the major hotels have Internet facilities, in their rooms or in the business center.

Most urban Omanis have an Internet connection at home, whether dial-up or more commonly DSL. It is less common to find this in the countryside. There is only one Internet service provider: OmanTel. It is relatively easy to subscribe to its services, although this entails a visit to its office and some form filling.

CONCLUSION

Omanis are warm and friendly people. Although their culture is complex, with quite different norms from those of the West, they welcome visitors to their country on the understanding that their values—religion, pride, modesty, and respect for people—are honored and respected.

Oman has always had important maritime links with the rest of the world, and throughout its history it has been influenced by foreign countries. Formally an absolute monarchy, it is a country that is both conservative and enlightened. This paradoxical situation only adds to its attractions for the outside world. Sultan Qaboos has taken positive steps to bring reform to his country, and is using its own natural resources with care to build a strong infrastructure. Oman may not be as rich in oil reserves as the neighboring Gulf countries, but the intelligent use of its funds is creating a firm foundation for the future.

Omanis value good relationships above time, and for the Western visitor this may take some getting used to. A relaxed attitude when it comes to the pace of both business and daily life is essential here. You may find the widespread bureaucracy—which is especially prevalent in government offices—frustrating and time-consuming, but the hospitality and generosity of the Omani people more than make up for this.

Oman is moving forward in terms of economic growth, while retaining the values and social ties that bind its people both to each other and to their country. It seems to have found an almost perfect balance of modernity and traditional life.

Further Reading

Agius, Dionisius. *Seafaring in the Arabian Gulf and Oman*. London: Kegan Paul International, 2005.

Al-Hinai, Abdulrahman Bin Ali. *Ceremonies and Celebrations of Oman*. London: Garnet Publishing, 2000.

Barth, Fredrick. *Sohar: Culture and Society in an Omani Town*. Baltimore: John Hopkins University Press, 1975.

Carter, J.R.L. *Tribes in Oman*. London: Immel Publishing, 1982.

Issac, Michael. *A Historical Atlas of Oman*. New York: Rosen Publishing Group, 2004.

Morris, Jan. *Sultan in Oman*. London: Sickle Moon Books, 2004.

Peyton, W.D. *Old Oman*. London: Stacey International, 2001.

Risso, Patricia. *Oman and Muscat: An Early Modern History*. London: Macmillan, 1986.

Stienbing, William H. Jr. *Uncovering the Past: A History of Archaeology*. Oxford: Oxford University Press, 1994.

Wilkinson, John Craven. *Water and Tribal Settlement in Southeast Arabia: A Study of the Aflaj of Oman*. Oxford: Clarendon Press, 1977.

Complete Arabic: The Basics. New York: Living Language, 2005.

In-Flight Arabic. New York: Living Language, 2001.

Index

Acknowledgments

For Cyrus, Isa, and Layla. Thank you for your love, support, and patience while I wrote this book.